Praise for *WHEN CHICKENHEADS COME HOME TO ROOST*

"When Chickenheads Come Home to Roost . . . is gaining nationwide acclaim for adding a fresh, idiosyncratic point of view—the voice of a new generation—to the oft-debated saga. Painstakingly straddling the line which separates street smarts from book intelligence, Morgan offers 240 pages worth of commentary on what it is like for a Black woman to come of age, Gen-X style. . . . While most Gen-Xers claim to be 'keepin' it real,' Morgan's new book instead shows that she's making the conscious choice to 'keep it right.' And not only by flipping and bouncing words and phrases that reflect today's popular culture, this new age feminist shows and proves that the day in which James Brown screams 'it's a man's world' might be finally coming to a dawn."

—Michael J. Rochon, *The Philadelphia Tribune*

"A debut collection of impassioned essays, written in poetic, flowing prose. . . . Fresh and articulate. Steadily perceptive, shrewdly provocative."

—*Kirkus Reviews*

"[Morgan] brings a powerful voice to concerns of modern black women."

—Vanessa Bush, *Booklist*

"As is the case with a lot of Morgan's work, *Chickenheads* remains unafraid to 'go there' around a few touchy issues. . . . [The book] will definitely engender passionate discussions among readers. . . . Regardless of how interpreted, you gotta give it up to this 'yardie gyal' from the Bronx who's brave enough to put her ideas out there so that the rest of us home-grrrls can all together start climbing toward wholeness."

—*Honey*

"Whether one agrees with Morgan or not, the sister definitely makes you think."

—Ronda Racha Penrice, *Rap Pages*

"A journalist by trade and outspoken black feminist by inclination, Joan Morgan has style to burn. . . . When Morgan brings it, she's funny, fierce, and yes feminist. . . . Morgan insists that the hip-hop generation can set its own goals—emotional, spiritual, social and political. Time to move on, and Morgan's leading the way."

—Cindy Fuchs, *Philadelphia City Paper*

"It's refreshing to see Morgan add racial dynamics to the gender-politics debate. . . . This book is a postmodern *Waiting to Exhale*—a romantic melodrama for all the black women who are beautiful, smart, accomplished and not apologizing for any man who can't get his act together. . . . Morgan is a credible independent spirit and autonomous woman."

—Caille Millner, *San Jose Mercury News*

"Joan Morgan has undertaken the necessary and painstaking task of navigating the world of Black Male/Female relationships. You go Joan! I saw myself in this book. Thank you for making me stop and think and reciprocate love."

—Ananda Lewis, television personality

"Everything you want to know about the sisters—and then some."

—Sean "Puffy" Combs

"Joan Morgan writes with passion, pain, and a charming playfulness about the fun and games of African-American life in the '90s."

—Nelson George, author of *Hip Hop America*

"Strong, soft, wise, and right on the beat with much flava to savor."

—Fab 5 Freddy

when chickenheads come home to roost

a hip-hop feminist breaks it down

joan morgan

simon & schuster paperbacks
new york london toronto sydney

SIMON & SCHUSTER PAPERBACKS
Rockefeller Center
1230 Avenue of the Americas
New York, NY 10020

SIMON & SCHUSTER PAPERBACKS and colophon are registered
trademarks of Simon & Schuster, Inc.

Designed by Chris Welch
Manufactured in the United States of America

7   9   10   8   6

The Library of Congress has cataloged the
hardcover edition as follows:
Morgan, Joan.
When chickenheads come home to roost: my life as a
hip-hop feminist / Joan Morgan.
p.   cm.
Includes bibliographical references and index.
1. Morgan, Joan.   2. Afro-American women—Biography.
3. Feminists—United States—Biography.   4. Afro-American
women—Social conditions.   5. Afro-American—
Civil rights.   I. Title.   II. Title: When chickenheads come
home to roost.
E185.86.M63   1999
973'.0496073'0092—dc21
[b]   98-50135   CIP

ISBN-13: 978-0-684-82262-4
ISBN-10:   0-684-82262-8
ISBN-13: 978-0-684-86861-5 (Pbk)
ISBN-10:   0-684-86861-X (Pbk)

Portions of "from fly-girls to bitches and hos" were originally
published in Vibe. Reprintd with permission.

Excerpt on p. 105:
Reprinted with the permission of Simon & Schuster, Inc.
from Acts of Faith by Iyanla Vanzant.
Copyright © 1993 by Iyanla Vanzant.

acknowledgments

Thanks and praises to God for love unconditional and my ancestors whose shoulders I stand on. Grandma Emily, Grandma Rachel, Great-grandma Jane, Grandpa Frank, Aunt Amy, Uncle Leroy walked close by and reminded me what I was made of. Maferefun Eggun. Maferefun Yemoja for giving me a crown at the beginning of this journey and the courage to wear it by the end. Modupues Iya Mi. Okun Shina. Maferefun Gbogbo Orisa for not only the love and strength you gave but the angels you sent to assist me: My editor, Sarah Baker, whose belief in this project was admirably unwavering—especially in the face of my self-doubt. I could not have done this without you. My agent, Sarah Lazin, who knew long before I did that there was a book inside me—waiting. The Morgan and Lawson families, who taught me how to fight and loved me through my battles. I love you immensely. My godmothers Judith Brabham and Stephanie Weaver for their continued support and examples of good character and dignity. My Ocha Family, for their prayers.

Special thanks to *Social Text, Essence,* and *Vibe* magazines; Ozzie's Coffee Shop in Park Slope (for current and caffeine); Marc and Jenny Baptiste, Jeffrey Woodley, Terrie Williams, Kim Hendrickson, and April Barton.

Mad love to the host of kind folk who fed me creatively, emotionally, and literally: Zahara and Malik Abdur-Razzaq, Mrs. Genevieve Hall Duncan, Keith Clinkscales, Alan Ferguson, Sophia Chang, Orgyln Clarke, Rebecca Williams, Charles Stone, Lisa Leone, Jac Benson, Chris Lighty, Raquel Cepeda, Fab 5 Freddy, Beth Ann Hardison, Carolyn Jones, Akissi Britton, Ed Lovelace, Kevin Powell, Audrey Edwards, Yvette Russell, Nelson George, Nadine Sutherland, and Gingi.

Malcolm love, I thank you for making the light at the end of the tunnel shine brighter than ever before.

Finally my eternal gratitude to all of the sistas I interviewed for this book. Your courage and generosity fortifies and inspires me. I will never stop telling our stories.

For my mother,
Maud Morgan.
The wind beneath my wings.

contents

"Who are you?" said the Caterpillar.

Alice replied, rather shyly, "I—I hardly know, Sir, . . . at least I know who I was when I got up this morning, but I think I must have changed several times since then."

—*Lewis Carroll*, Alice's Adventures in Wonderland

intro.
dress up

It started with a dress. A hot little thing. A spaghetti-strapped Armani number, with a skintight bodice and a long flowing skirt, in that shade of orange that black girls do the most justice. I bought it in La-La Land precisely because it reminded me of New York in the seventies, with its sexy sistas (girls with names like Pokie, Nay-Nay, Angela, and Robin) and those leotard and dance skirt sets they used to rock back in the day. This was back when I was a shorty with cherries for breasts and absolutely no ass to speak of. I used to sit on our tenement stoop mesmerized by the way those flimsy little tops knew how to hug a tittie in all the right places, or the way a proper Bronx Girl Switch (two parts Switch to one part Bop) could make the skirts move like waves. Wide-eyed, I watched regla project girls transform into Black Moseses capable of parting seas of otherwise idle Negros.

And I couldn't wait to be one.

The opportunity presented itself two decades later. The Crayola-colored ladies of Ntozake Shange's famous choreopoem *for colored girls who have considered suicide/ when the rainbow is enuf* had just turned twenty and various factions of black New York turned out to help

17

them celebrate. The sight of the Niggerati, R-n-B weave divas, church ladies, bohemians, and ultra-Nubians milling about outside the theater made for a delectable pretheater aperitif. And folks showed up early—in complete defiance of C.P. Time—in order to fully imbibe.

The dress was my personal tribute. So when Dude called out an appreciative, "Heeyyy lady in orange," flashing all thirty-two of his pearly whites, I couldn't help it. I had to slay him. Fancying myself to be none other than Shange's Sechita, the *deliberate coquette with orange butterflies and aqua sequins* floating between her breasts, I threw a little more hip in the switch than usual, and smiled back half as long but just as hard. Dramatic yes, but hey, the day had been a long time coming.

Few hissy fits can compare to the one I threw twenty years ago when my mom announced she was taking her husband and not her precocious woman-child to see Shange's play. I'd been transfixed by the poster since the first day it went up on our community center's wall. Afro-puffed and arms akimbo, I'd stare at it every day, struck by the poster-woman's sad, sad eyes and the eeriness of the title scribbled in child-like graffiti across an imaginary tenement wall.

It didn't matter that I didn't know a damn thing about suicide. Death, yes—since departed colored girls are part of the ghetto's given—but none of them had left in ways as exotic as checking out on their own volition. But I reasoned that the play had something to do with being black, female, and surviving—and those were intuitive if not conscious concerns for any ten-year-old colored girl growing up in the South Bronx 'round 1975.

So convinced was I that this play held some crucial part of me, my moms's decision to take my father constituted high gender treason. I acted out accordingly. I pleaded and cajoled, bawled and whined, and when that proved to be of no avail, I employed the pouty silent treatment. Even when my moms firmly reminded me that no one in our house believed the rod spoiled the child, I refused to let it go. I sang the Five Stairsteps' "O-o-h child things are going to get easier" over and over again—attitudinal and loud—until I was two seconds shy of an ass-whooping.

My obsession with *for colored girls* . . . carried over well into adulthood, long after I snuck into the adult section of the public library, stole the book, and fell in love with words and images I didn't quite understand. It remained among my favorites as I grew older and sought balmy remedies for tempestuous emotions about black men, women, and myself. Seeing it performed was always cathartic and I never missed an opportunity —except for that first run on Broadway in 1975.

I've long since forgiven my mother, of course. In my pre-adolescent selfishness I failed to see that she too was a colored girl. The play held crucial parts of her —parts she needed to share with her husband and not her ten-year-old daughter.

Like so many women of her time, my mother was deeply immersed in the exciting, frightening, and feminist process of becoming herself. Receiving her G.E.D., becoming a full-time college student, and eventually a registered nurse enabled her to shed the restrictive costumes of domestic, mother, and wife. She became, as *Ntozake Shange* literally means, "a woman who walks through the world with her own things. One who walks like a lion."

Such transformation requires new spiritual and emotional attire. Her newfound confidence (not to mention emotional and financial independence from my father) was hard-earned—evidenced by the copious, midnight tears she never knew I saw. But over the years I watched her painfully pull apart and successfully re-stitch the pieces of her life. For my mother and black women like her, Shange's play gave their experiences a legitimacy and a voice it would take me years to comprehend.

So many of those women were there, gathered outside the Henry Street Theatre on that glorious early summer day, anxious to witness the twentieth-anniversary run. Like me I suppose they were reminiscing about where this play fit into their lives.

As the curtain rose and the actresses took their places on stage, I was filled with the same anticipation I felt that night twenty years ago, when I'd waited up long past bedtime for my parents' return, anxious for the blow-by-blow that would reveal the secrets of black womanhood.

I didn't get it back then. Daddy's response—little more than a grunt—told me nothing. Mom's response was simply that I was too young to know.

And I didn't get it in 1995. I'd come into the theater hoping to finally feel what my mother must have over two decades ago. I wanted Shange's language to arm me with the awesome power of self-definition. I left realizing this was impossible. As much as I appreciated the artistic, cultural, and historical significance of this moment it wasn't mine to claim.

As a child of the post–Civil Rights, post-feminist, post-soul hip-hop generation, my struggle songs consisted of the same notes but they were infused with distinctly different rhythms. What I wanted was a *for colored girls* . . . of my own. The problem was that I was waiting around for someone else to write it.

This complacency is typical of my generation. Our ancestors' struggles, accomplishments, and errors may have blessed us with an acute sense of analysis, but privilege and comfort make us slow to initiate change. It's up to our elders, we figure, to create a bandwagon fly enough for us to jump on. Unfortunately, the problems don't go away while we wait. Instead, racism, sexism, poverty, inadequate education, escalating rates of incarceration, piss-poor health conditions, drugs, and violence continue to corrupt the quality of our lives every day. Relying on older heads to redefine the struggle to encompass our generation's issues is not only lazy but dangerous.

Mad love and respect to black foremothers (like Angela Davis, bell hooks, Pearl Cleage, Ntozake Shange, and Audre Lorde, to name a few) who passionately articulated their struggles and suggested agendas (imperfect or not) for black female empowerment, but these sistas did their due. The enormous task of saving our lives falls on nobody else's shoulders but ours. Consider our foremothers' contributions a bad-ass bolt of cloth. We've got to fashion the gear to our own liking.

This book, in part, was an effort to combat my own complacency. I wrote it because I honestly believe that the only way sistas can begin to experience empowerment on all levels—spiritual, emotional, financial, and political—is to understand who we are. We have to be willing to take an honest look at ourselves—and then tell the truth about it.

Much of what we'll see will be fly as hell. A lot will be painful and trifling. Like Langston Hughes said, *We are beautiful but we are ugly too. The tom-tom laughs. The tom-tom cries.* But only when we've told the truth about ourselves—when we've faced the fact that we are often complicit in our oppression—will we be able to take full responsibility for our lives. The only way we'll ever know what to do about 70 percent of our children being born to single mothers,[1] the state of mutual disrespect that plagues our intimate relationships, the bitches and hos that live among us, or the chickenhead that lurks inside us all is to "keep it real"—without compromise.

And I'm not going to lie; the process is often terrifying. While writing this book, I went from sharing our funky, deep woman's shit with my homegirls to putting it down on paper for general public consumption. Trust me, all my years of writing articles dealing with men's sexism and racism was easy by comparison. I can't give enough love to the chorus of sista voices that embarked with me on this journey. Whether they were formal parts of my research groups, or strangers who kicked it with me in coffee shops their exchanges served as beacons, encouraging me to travel to places I would have found too frightening to explore alone in the dark. For that I'm forever thankful.

Trying to address our diversity was equally as stressful. How in Oshun's name to capture the nose-ringed/caesared/weaved up/Gucci-Prada-DKNY down/ultra-Nubian/alternative-bohemian/beats-loving/smooth-jazz-playing magic of us was something I couldn't begin to fathom. What got me through (besides the unconditional love and support of my mama, godparents, editor, fam, and friends) was remembering some advice I once gave Kim, a former student of mine.

Kim took an acting class I taught at the predominantly rich, white prep school we'd both attended. She was understandably anxious to find a scene where she could *be a black girl* (instead of a black girl trying to add her own mocha flava to a role clearly written for someone white, which, given our alma mater's make-up, happened a lot). She suggested Shange's poem *somebody almost walked off wid alla my stuff* and asked if I thought she could handle it. Not only did I think she could, I was thrilled by the prospect. Kim was evolving into a fierce young actor and the monologue was one of my favorites.

Her first rendition attempted to parrot the voice immortalized on the *colored girls . . .* sound track, replete with her own sassy inflections. She was a veritable eye-rollin', smart-talkin', finger-snappin' Miss Thang, but she wasn't believable. What I wanted in lieu of the black girl attitude was *her* truth. Kim was raised on hip-hop, not jazz or the blues, and she didn't know nothing about Sun-Ra, Dew City, or Mr. Louisiana Hot Link. In order for her to possess the piece and make it hers she was going to have to infuse it with her own voice and experiences.

I gave her two pieces of advice. The first was to tell her truth and stop worrying about encompassing the entire spectrum of black female identity. The second was to start with what she knew. After a few difficult and teary-eyed attempts, Mr. Louisiana Hot Link became the rapper D-nice; the neck-rollin', finger-snappin' anger gave way to the soft-spoken, vulnerable, fearful sound of a sixteen-year-old heart breaking for the very first time. It was both fantastic and powerful.

Writing this book has given me much compassion

for how difficult this was for Kim. In a society of ever-shifting identity politics, I was asking this sixteen-year-old to sift through so many conflicting interpretations of femaleness and blackness and free her voice. In order to do this she was going to have to liberate it from the stranglehold of media stereotypes—the pathetic SheNayNay impersonations of black male comedians, the talk-to-the-hand Superwomen, the video-hos, crackheads, and lazy welfare queens—that obscure so much of who we are. And she was going to have to push her foremothers' voices far enough away to discover her own.

I knew that I needed to follow my own advice if I was going to write this book. Trying to capture the voice of all that is young black female was impossible. My goal, instead, was to tell my truth as best I could from my vantage point on the spectrum. And then get you to talk about it. This book by its lonesome won't give you the truth. Truth is what happens when your cumulative voices fill in the breaks, provide the re-mixes, and rework the chorus.

Believe me, I'll be listening for it.

In the meantime, I'm kicking it off with what I know.

the f-word

O n our quests to create ourselves we brown girls play dress up. What is most fascinating about this ritual of imitation is what we choose to mimic—what we reach for in our mothers' closets. We move right on past the unglamorous garb of our mothers' day-to-day realities—the worn housedresses or beat-up slippers—and reach instead for the intimates. Slip our sassy little selves into their dressiest of dresses and sexiest of lingerie like being grown is like Christmas or Kwanzaa and can't come fast enough.

Then we practice the deadly art of attitude—rollin' eyes,

necks, and hips in mesmerizing synchronization, takin' out imaginary violators with razor-sharp tongues. Perhaps to our ingenuous eyes transforming ourselves into invincible Miss Thangs is the black woman's only armature against the evils of the world.

Interestingly enough, we do not imitate our mothers at their weakest or most vulnerable. Shedding silent midnight tears, alone and afraid. That we don't do until much later, when we are fully grown, occasionally trippin' and oblivious to our behavior's origins.

It took years to realize that the same process was true of my feminism. For a very long time I was a black woman completely unaware that I faced the world in my mother's clothes . . .

I became a black feminist writer in the least feminist of ways. It happened one night in Harlem, up on Sugar Hill with a man the goddess had thrown in my path to grant me the sufferice I thought I needed to become a real woman. I was the young lover of a celebrated griot of black post-modernism, an icon of eighties black bohemia. He was a seductively brilliant brother with limited emotional skills, a penchant for younger women, and a Pygmalion obsession of legendary notoriety.

At twenty-four, I'd already been an assistant manager at a major retail store, an aspiring actress, and a very good teacher, but I still had no idea what I wanted to be when I grew up. So I stepped into my lover's life like I arrived in Harlem—willing and pliable—fresh outta lockdown in South Bronx soul prisons and armed with fly-girl attitude and wanna-be bohemian desire. In short, I was as ghetto a Galatea as you could get.

The night I became a black feminist writer was so like every other night that the details are rendered indiscernible. For poetry's sake I would like to say it started with one of those tender post-coital moments, brown limb entwined with brown limb, discussing the implications of wildin', race, and rape in the Central Park Jogger case. This is unlikely. My lover was not tender and we were not particularly compatible.

More likely than not, the conversation took place over the phone, with him in his space and me in mine, enjoying the magic of an unobstructed Sugar Hill view. To my right, Yankee Stadium and the rest of the Boogie-Down served as backdrop for the nocturnal adventures of the Polo Grounds. On the left was Amsterdam, then Broadway, painted colorful and loud by the nonstop traffic of an ever-growing Dominican presence. But I was probably looking straight ahead, down the block, past my lover's building, past Harlem, Central Park, the Empire State Building, and somewhere past that— the rest of the world. And that's when I told him that *writing an article about the racial implications of the Central Park Jogger case without discussing gender was, like, bananas 'cause yes the coverage was racist, but that doesn't change the fact that the woman was raped and probably by some brown boys. I mean damn, wasn't anybody gonna say she wasn't a victim becuz she was white, she was a victim becuz she was a woman and what did he think, that if I was a black investment banker who happened to be in the park that night I wouldn't be raped 'cause homeboys woulda been like, "Naw we can't hit it 'cuz she a sista"? And if it was a sista lying there where would we be 'cuz talking about niggas and sexism is like, mad taboo. So maybe, just maybe while we're busy being mad at the white folks we could also take a minute to acknowledge that sexism and violence against women occurs in our community too and our men are no better or worse than anybody else's.*

My lover's kindness lay in the generosity of his talent, his unfailing ability to pull out diamonds where others see only coal. He called his editor early that morning and told her about my midnight rave. When she asked if I could write, he doggedly ignored my lack of experience, cast aside the fact that I'd never expressed as much as passing desire, and said simply, "Yes. She can." Thirty-six hours later I turned in my first feature for a national weekly paper.

The piece got considerable play and I was re-christened Joan Morgan——Black Feminist Writer. It took a year of being published before I would call myself a writer. It took that long to figure out I had something valuable to say. My lover's work was done when I did, and we went our separate ways.

Coming out as a black feminist, however, was another matter entirely.

Feminism claimed me long before I claimed it. The foundation was laid by women who had little use for the word. Among them the three country women—mother, daughter, and sister—who brought me into this world sans hospital, electricity, or running water. (My father was off doing whatever it is island men do while their women give birth to girl children.) Shortly after, my mother left Jamaica to see for herself that the streets of the Bronx were not paved with gold. They were paved with things more frightening than she could have imagined. So she armed her children with the King's English, good character, and explicit instructions to kick the ass of any knucklehead stupid enough to come for us. In the meantime, she cleaned white folks' homes, put herself and two kids through college, and proceeded to travel the world.

There were others. The mothers of friends. The grande dame Genevieve survived burying a husband, three children, and a daughter-in-law and taught us a woman commands a great deal of power when she remains, above all else, a lady. Sassy Aunt Claire* kicked a drug addiction square in the ass to resume her perpetual love affair with life. Lois's fierce spirit was the harness that held her child back from the grave, until cancer caused her to slip and fall into her own.

* Not her real name.

And of course, Marvelous Melba aka Grand Diva Emeritus who loved magic and flowers and sensual things and was always down to share a few secrets over a good cappuccino. I did not know that feminism is what you called it when black warrior women moved mountains and walked on water. Growing up in their company, I considered these things ordinary.

The spirits of these women were nowhere to be found in the feminism I discovered in college. Feminists on our New England campus came in two flavas—both variations of vanilla. The most visible were the braless, butch-cut, anti-babes, who seemed to think the solution to sexism was reviling all things male (except, oddly enough, their clothing and mannerisms) and sleeping with each other. They used made up words like "womyn," "femynists," and threw mad shade if you asked them directions to the "Ladies' Room." The others—straight and more femme—were all for the liberation of women as long as it did not infringe on their sense of entitlement. They felt their men should *share* the power to oppress. They were the spiritual descendants of the early suffragettes and absolutely not to be trusted.

This is not to say that our differences were so great that the wave of feminist activism on campus left me totally unaffected. I stuck my toes in the water. I was adamantly pro-choice, attended speak-outs against rape and domestic violence, and made sure to vote for candidates who paid lip-service to equal pay for equal work, protecting planned parenthood, legalized abortion, and quality child care. But feminism definitely felt like white women's shit.

White girls don't call their men "brothers" and that made their struggle enviably simpler than mine. Racism and the will to survive it creates a sense of intra-racial loyalty that makes it impossible for black women to turn our backs on black men—even in their ugliest and most sexist of moments. I needed a feminism that would allow us to continue loving ourselves *and* the brothers who hurt us without letting race loyalty buy us early tombstones.

Being the bastion of liberal education it was, the university's curriculum did expose me to feminists of color. (Unfortunately this happened far more frequently in African-American Studies courses than it did in Women's Studies). Dedicated professors—male and female—exhumed the voices of Sojourner Truth, Ida B. Wells, Frances Harper, and Mary Church Terrell and let me know that black women had been making it their bidness to speak out against sexism and racism for over 250 years. (That it took almost twelve years of formal education to find out our contribution to African-American history was more than Harriet Tubman or Coretta Scott King made me seriously question if only white folks were guilty of revisionist history.) Discovering the works of Alice Walker, Angela Davis, Audre Lorde, Paula Giddings, and bell hooks—black women who claimed the f-word boldly—not only enabled me to understand the complex and often complicit relationship between both isms; it empowered me with language to express the unique oppression that comes with being colored and a woman.

I was eternally grateful, but I was not a feminist.

When I thought about feminism—women who were living and breathing it daily—I thought of white women or black female intellectuals. Academics. Historians. Authors. Women who had little to do with my everyday life. The sistas in my immediate proximity grew up in the 'hood, summered in the Hamptons, swapped spit on brightly lit Harlem corners, and gave up more than a li'l booty in Ivy League dorms. They were ghetto princesses with a predilection for ex–drug dealers. They got their caesars cut at the barbershop and perms at the Dominican's uptown. They were mack divas who rolled wit posses fifteen bitches deep and lived for Kappa beach parties, the Garage, the Roxy, and all things hip-hop. Black feminists were some dope sistas, respected elders most def, but they were not my contemporaries. They were not crew. And for most of my twenties, crew was what mattered.

But I was also a twenty-four-year-old who'd begun writing highly volatile articles on black male sexism and the conspiracy of protective silence that surrounds it. If I wasn't going to call myself a feminist, I'd better come up with something. Folks like to know what to call you when they're cussing you out.

Thanks to Marc Christian* I found this out with a quickness.

Marc Christian was a sorcerer with a loft on the borderline of black Harlem and El Barrio. A photographer by trade, he was haunted by visions of unearthed black beauty, so he made a business outta making black folks beautiful. He called it "reminding them who they are." In his unspectacular loft, with its dingy white walls and worn wood floors, Marc Christian worked magic on the regular. Boxers with badly bludgeoned faces were given the regality of Zulu warriors; nude

* Not his real name.

brown girls with Hottentot asses made love to his lenses like they grew up finding themselves in *Vogue;* ciphers of old drunk men recovered bits of spirits long ago sent swimming in Wild Irish Rose bottles. All he asked in return was for a little bit of their souls. He usually got it. Marc Christian was highly skilled in the art of seduction and a very pretty nigga. So when he called talkin' 'bout, "Yeah, baby, I read the article, your stunning debut. Now come bring your fine ass over here so I can talk to you 'bout this heavy shit you gettin' into," I dropped everything and jumped in a cab. Like most folks, I was defenseless against his juju.

Truth be told I couldn't wait to step into Marc Christian's loft with some semblance of a creative identity. I remembered the many times I sat awestruck and envious while he and my lover parleyed with various members of New York's Niggerati. I was hardly a member of that illustrious set, but for once "the work" was mine. I wanted to kick it with Marc up on his roof where the world was spread out like a humongous smorgasbord that extended as far as spirit, will, and appetite would take you. Of course, getting him to stop working would probably require some *brujeria* of my own but I was determined to have his undivided attention. As soon as I walked in the front door I knew this would not be the case. Marc Christian had company. Three men. Strangers who were expecting me.

Foolishly, I'd forgotten Marc Christian occasionally satiated his hunger for drama by mixing highly incendiary elements. At his prompting, each one of the men had read the article and was prepared to do battle. I had no choice but to go for mine.

"So you're the sista who wrote the article?" asked the first, in a tone less curious than caustic. He was young. A Latino homeboy with ghetto allegiances and bohemian aspirations. He and his compadre—a Queens cutie with Trini roots—were Marc Christian's newest apprentices. As fellow creative spirits they gave me my props for "getting the work out there." They were upset, however, that my article didn't emphasize the impact of the rape on their lives.

It was a valid point. The city's current climate was undeniably ill. The rape became a self-righteous hook that racists conveniently hung their prejudices on. Brothers all over were forced to watch powerless as the media reduced them to savages and white women gripped their pocketbooks even harder in fear. Faced with these brothers' pain, it was easy to see why a critical article written by a black woman for a predominantly white paper felt not only traitorous but hurtful. Despite my convictions my Black Male Empathy Reflex was kickin' like a motherfucka.

Just as I began to question my ability to deal with such obviously divided loyalties Stranger #3 took center stage. He was in his early forties, some kinda horn player and bedecked in sixties attire, down to his ill-fitting high-waters. "Alla this was bullshit!" he declared ceremoniously and advised the young ones to step aside so he could "set the record straight."

Pausing only to hear the leftover conga beats that still played in his head, Money black-power-pimp strolled across the floor and kicked it faux Last Poets.

My siss-tah, don't you seee?
 You are be-ing yoused.
 Thisss is how the cracker da-feets
  the BLACK man every-time.
  He captures the minds
   of our women
   and uses them
  to speak out a-gainst us.
  Don't you seeee.
   My siss-tah
 You are a tool of the white man . . .

It's been said Marc Christian could sometimes read minds so I offered him a piece of my own. *Alright, you've had your fun. Now why don't you reel your boy back in before he plays himself. You know damn well those wanna-be revolutionary theatrics are wasted on folks who were only around for five years of the sixties . . .* His only reply was the hint of a grin.

Unchecked, the asshole who considered himself the heavy artillery continued.

> *My siss-tah my siss-tah my siss-tah*
> *Do ya even like men?*
> *'cuz ya could be one a dem*
> *funny girls*
> *(UH-HUH, UH-HUH)*
> *then in that case you'd need something else to save ya*
> *(ha-ha)*

He said this of course, this little bit of a man (with feet and hands smaller than nobody's business), as if I'd consider being mistaken for a lesbian an insult instead of an inaccuracy. For a second I couldn't tell what pissed me off more, the assumption that any woman who is willing to call a black man out on his shit *must* be eating pussy or his depiction of me as a brainwashed

Sappho, waving the American flag in one hand and a castrated black male penis in the other. As it turns out, there wasn't time to decide; he finished his malediction by throwing down the gauntlet.

> *Ya know Marc Christian?*
> *Ya know what we got here?*
> *my brotha*
> *We got us one dem*
> *FEM-in-ists.*
> *Are you a feminist*
> *my siss-tah? . . .*

And there it was, the f-word all up in my face daring me to blanket myself in the yarns I'd spun to justify my rejection. *Go on, girl. Deny me and tell this fool about cha lover and the butch-cut white girls and see if he gives a fuck.* Searching for a viable, less volatile alternative I did a quick mental check of the popular epithets. Strong Black Woman. Womanist. Warrior Woman. Nubian Queen. Bitch. Gangsta Bitch. Bitches With Problems. Hos With Attitude. None of them offered even the hint of protection.

Finally, I realized that in the face of sexism it didn't matter what I called myself. Semantics would not save me from the jerks I was bound to run into if I continued to do this for a living nor would it save women from the violence of teenage boys who suffered from their own misconceptions of power and manhood. If I truly believed that the empowerment of the black community had to include its women, or that sexism stood stubbornly in the way of black men and women loving each other or sistas loving themselves, if I acknowledged this both in print and in person then in any sexist's eyes I was a feminist. Once I recognized these manifestations of black-on-black love as the dual heartbeats of black feminism, I was purged of doubt. I accepted his challenge with confidence.

Since my sexual preference could not be of any relevance to you, whatcha really wanna know is how I feel about brothas. It's simple. I love black men like I love no other. And I'm not talking sex or aesthetics, I'm talking about loving y'all enough to be down for the drama—stomping anything that threatens your existence. Now only a fool loves that hard without asking the same in return. So yeah, I demand that black men fight sexism with the same passion they battle racism. I want you to annihilate anything that endangers sistas' welfare—including violence against women—because my survival walks hand in hand with yours. So, my brotha, *if loving y'all fiercely and wanting it back makes me a feminist then I'm a feminist. So be it.*

As our cab made its way through the Harlem night, I'd asked Marc Christian if luring unsuspecting friends into the dens of wolves was a regular practice. He replied with a severity I'd never seen from him. "The article was damn good, but you are better. Your work comes from your heart and the truth is some powerful shit. That's black magic. When people find out you got that they gonna keep trying to tear you apart. You already know you got skills. Tonight was about getting your *cojónes*."

The moment catapulted me across time and the bridge, back to my family's small South Bronx apartment. I'd run upstairs one day to tell my mother about a bigger, older girl who kept threatening to kick my ass becuz our family dressed in clean clothes, spoke decent English, and dared not to be on welfare. My attempts to ignore her only infuriated her more and that day she pushed the issue by shoving me. I told my mother in the hopes she would go downstairs and hit her (and if need be her mother) or tell her to leave me alone. Instead, she said, "If she hits you again, fight her—pick up something if you have to—but if I hear you stood there and let her beat your ass I'm gonna come downstairs and beat yours." And she went back to whatever she was doing. Minutes later, my nemesis hit me again, and I beat the child bloody.

"So how did I do, Marc?" I asked in a voice that belonged more to the ten-year-old girl telling her mom the details of her battle than the young woman sitting next to him. "You mean the *cojónes?*" he said and let out a sorcerer's laugh that charmed even the gypsy cab driver who'd been impatiently waiting for my departure. "Baby, you gonna be just fine. You got a bigger dick than most niggas I know." And with that I said good night and tucked my friend's departing words safely away in my treasure chest of talismans.

hip-hop
feminist

Much had changed in my life by the time a million black men marched in Washington. I no longer live in Harlem. The decision had less to do with gunshot lullabies, dead bodies 'round the corner, or the pre-adolescents safe-sexing it in my stairwells—running consensual trains on a twelve-year-old girl whose titties and ass grew faster than her self-esteem—and more to do with my growing desensitization to it all. As evidenced by the zombie-like stare in my neighbors' eyes, the ghetto's dues for emotional immunity is high. And I knew better than to test its capacity for contagion.

So I broke out. Did a Bronx girl's unthinkable and moved to Brooklyn—where people had kids and dogs and gardens and shit. And a park called Prospect contained ol' West Indian men who reminded me of yet another home and everything good about my father.

It is the Bronx that haunts me, though. There a self, long deaded, roams the Concourse, dressed in big bamboo earrings and flare-legged Lees, guarding whatever is left of her memories. I murdered her. Slowly. By sipping miasmic cocktails of non-ghetto dreams laced with raw ambition. I had to. She would have clung so tightly to recollections of monkey bars, sour pickles, and BBQ Bontons, slow dances to "Always and Forever," and tongue kisses *coquito* sweet—love that existed despite the insanities and rising body counts—that escape would have been impossible.

It is the Bronx, not Harlem that calls me back. Sometimes she is the singsong cadences of my family's West Indian voices. Or the childhood memories of girls I once called friends. Sistas who refused the cocktail and had too many babies way too young. Sistas who saw welfare, bloodshed, dust, then crack steal away any traces of youth from their smiles.

Theirs are the spirits I see darting between the traffic and the La Marqueta vibes of Fordham Road. Their visitations dog my equanimity, demanding I explain why this "feminism thing" is relevant to any of their lives. There are days I cannot. I'm too busy wondering what relevance it has in my own.

. . . And then came October 16, the day Louis Farrakhan declared that black men would finally stand up and seize their rightful place as leaders of their communities. . . . It wasn't banishment from the march that was so offensive—after all, black women have certainly convened at our share of

closed-door assemblies. It was being told to stay
home and prepare food for our warrior kings. What
infuriated progressive black women was that the
rhetoric of protection and atonement was just a
seductive mask for good old-fashioned sexism. . . .

Kristal Brent-Zooks, "A Manifesto of Sorts for a New
Black Feminist Movement," *The New York Times Magazine*[1]

The "feminist" reaction to the Million Man March
floored me. Like a lot of folks, I stayed home to watch
the event. My phone rang off the hook—sista friends
as close as round the corner and as far away as Jamaica
moved by the awesome sight of so many black men of
different hues, classes, and sexual orientations gathered
together *peacefully* for the sole purpose of bettering
themselves. The significance of the one group in this
country most likely to murder each other—literally
take each other out over things as trifling as colors or
stepping on somebody's sneakers—was not lost on us.
In fact, it left us all in tears.

Still, as a feminist, I could hardly ignore that my
reaction differed drastically from many of my feminist
counterparts. I was not mad. Not mad at all. Perhaps
it was because growing up sandwiched between two
brothers blessed me with an intrinsic understanding of

the sanctity of male and female space. (Maintaining any semblance of harmony in our too-small apartment meant figuring out the times my brothers and I could share space—and the times we could not—with a quickness.)

Perhaps it was because I've learned that loving brothers is a little like parenting—sometimes you gotta get all up in that ass. Sometimes you gotta let them figure it out *on their own terms*—even if it means they screw up a little. So while the utter idiocy inherent in a nineties black leader suggesting women stay home and make sandwiches for their men didn't escape me, it did not nullify the march's positivity either. It's called being able to see the forest *and* the trees.

Besides, I was desperately trying to picture us trying to gather a million or so sistas to march for the development of a new black feminist movement. Highly, highly unlikely. Not that there aren't black women out there actively seeking agendas of empowerment—be it personal or otherwise—but let's face it, sistas ain't exactly checkin' for the f-word.

When I told older heads that I was writing a book which explored, among other things, my generation of black women's precarious relationship with feminism, they looked at me like I was trying to re-invent the wheel. I got lectured ad nauseam about "the racism of the White Feminist Movement," "the sixties and the seventies," and "feminism's historic irrelevance to black folks." I was reminded of how feminism's ivory tower elitism excludes the masses. And I was told that black women simply "didn't have time for all that shit."

While there is undeniable truth in all of the above except the latter—*the shit* black women don't have time for is dying and suffering from exorbitant rates of solo parenting, domestic violence, drug abuse, incarceration, AIDS, and cancer—none of them really explain why we have no black feminist *movement*. Lack of college education explains why 'round-the-way girls aren't reading bell hooks. It does not explain why even the gainfully degreed (self included) would rather trick away our last twenty-five dollars on that new nineties black girl fiction (trife as some of it may be) than some of those good, but let's face it, laboriously academic black feminist texts.

White women's racism and the Feminist Movement may explain the justifiable bad taste the f-word leaves in the mouths of women who are over thirty-five, but for my generation they are abstractions drawn from someone else's history. And without the power of memories, these phrases mean little to nothing.

Despite our differences about the March, Brent-Zooks's article offered some interesting insights.

. . . Still, for all our double jeopardy about being black and female, progressive black women have yet to galvanize a mass following or to spark a concrete movement for social change. . . . Instead of picking up where Ida B. Wells left off, black women too often allow our efforts to be reduced to the anti-lynching campaigns of the Tupac Shakurs, the Mike Tysons, the O. J. Simpsons and the Clarence Thomases of the world. Instead of struggling with, and against, those who sanction injustice, too often we stoop beneath them, our backs becoming their bridges. . . .

Why do we remain stuck in the past? The answer has something to do with not just white racism but also our own fear of the possible, our own inability to imagine the divinity within ourselves. . . .[2]

I agree. At the heart of our generation's ambivalence about the f-word is black women's historic tendency to blindly defend any black man who seems to be under attack from white folks (men, women, media, criminal justice system, etc.). The fact that the brothers may very well be in the wrong and, in some cases, deserve to be buried *under* the jail is irrelevant—even if the victim is one of us. Centuries of being rendered helpless while racism, crime, drugs, poverty, depression, and violence robbed us of our men has left us misguidedly over-protective, hopelessly male-identified, and all too often self-sacrificing.

And yes, fear is part of the equation too, but I don't think it's a fear of the possible. Rather, it is the justifiable fear of what lies ahead for any black woman boldly proclaiming her commitment to empowerment—her sistas' or her own. Acknowledging the rampant sexism in our community, for example, means relinquishing the comforting illusion that black men and women are a unified front. Accepting that black men do not always reciprocate our need to love and protect is a terrifying thing, because it means that we are truly out there, *assed out* in a world rife with sexism and racism. And who the hell wants to deal with that?

Marc Christian was right. *Cojónes* became a necessary part of my feminist armature—but not for the reasons I would have suspected back then. I used to fear the constant accusations—career opportunism, race treason, collusion with "The Man," lesbianism—a lifetime of explaining what I am not. I dreaded the long, tedious conversations spent exorcising others of the stereotypes that tend to haunt the collective consciousness when we think of black women and the f-word—male basher, radical literary/academic black women in their forties and fifties who are pathetically separated from real life, burly dreadlocked/crew cut dykes, sexually adventurous lipstick-wearing bisexuals, victims. Even more frightening were the frequent solo conversations I spent exorcising them from my own head.

In time, however, all of that would roll off my back like water.

Cojónes became necessary once I discovered that mine was not a feminism that existed comfortably in the black and white of things. The precarious nature of my career's origins was the first indication. I got my start as a writer because I captured the sexual attention of a man who could make me one. It was not the first time my externals would bestow me with such favors. It certainly would not be the last.

My growing fatigue with talking about "the men" was the second. Just once, I didn't want to have to talk about "the brothers," "male domination," or "the patriarchy." I wanted a feminism that would allow me to explore who we are as women—not victims. One that claimed the powerful richness and delicious complexities inherent in being black girls now—sistas of the post—Civil Rights, post-feminist, post soul, hip-hop generation.

I was also looking for permission to ask some decidedly un-P.C. but very real questions:

Can you be a good feminist and admit out loud that there are things you kinda dig about patriarchy?

Would I be forced to turn in my "feminist membership card" if I confessed that suddenly waking up in a world free of gender inequities or expectations just might bug me out a little?

Suppose you don't want to pay for your own dinner, hold the door open, fix things, move furniture, or get intimate with whatever's under the hood of a car?

Is it foul to say that imagining a world where you could paint your big brown lips in the most decadent of shades, pile your phat ass into your fave micromini, slip your freshly manicured toes into four-inch fuck-me sandals and have not one single solitary man objectify—I mean roam his eyes longingly over all the intended places—is, like, a total drag for you?

Am I no longer down for the cause if I admit that while total gender equality is an interesting intellectual concept, it doesn't do a damn thing for me erotically? That, truth be told, men with too many "feminist" sensibilities have never made my panties wet, at least not like that reformed thug nigga who can make even the most chauvinistic of "wassup, baby" feel like a sweet, wet tongue darting in and out of your ear.

And how come no one ever admits that part of the reason women love hip-hop—as sexist as it is—is 'cuz all that in-yo-face testosterone makes our nipples hard?

Are we no longer good feminists, not to mention nineties supersistas, if the A.M.'s wee hours sometimes leave us tearful and frightened that achieving all our mothers wanted us to—great educations, careers, financial and emotional independence—has made us wholly undesirable to the men who are supposed to be our counterparts? Men whose fascination with chickenheads leave us convinced they have no interest in dating, let alone marrying, their equals?

And when one accuses you of being completely indecipherable there's really nothing to say 'cuz even you're not sure how you can be a feminist and insist he "respect you as a woman, treat you like a lady, and make you feel safe—like a li'l girl."

In short, I needed a feminism brave enough to fuck with the grays. And this was not my foremothers' feminism.

Ironically, reaping the benefits of our foremothers' struggle is precisely what makes their brand of feminism so hard to embrace. The "victim" (read women) "oppressor" (read men) model that seems to dominate so much of contemporary discourse (both black and white), denies the very essence of who we are.

We are the daughters of feminist privilege. The gains of the Feminist Movement (the efforts of black, white, Latin, Asian, and Native American women) had a tremendous impact on our lives—so much we often take it for granted. We walk through the world with a sense of entitlement that women of our mothers' generation could not begin to fathom. Most of us can't imagine our lives without access to birth control, legalized abortions, the right to vote, or many of the same educational and job opportunities available to men. Sexism may be a very real part of my life but so is the unwavering belief that there is no dream I can't pursue *and achieve* simply because "I'm a woman."

Rejecting the wildly popular notion that embracing the f-word entails nothing more than articulating victimization, for me, is a matter of personal and spiritual survival. Surviving the combined impact of racism and sexism on the daily means never allowing my writing to suggest that black women aren't more than a bunch of bad memories. We *are* more than the rapes survived by the slave masters, the illicit familial touches accompanied by whiskey-soured breath, or the acts of violence endured by the fists, knives, and guns of strangers. We are more than the black eyes and heart bruises from those we believed were friends.

Black women can no more be defined by the cumulative sum of our pain than blackness can be defined solely by the transgenerational atrocities delivered at the hands of American racism. Because black folks are more than the stench of the slave ship, the bite of the dogs, or the smoldering of freshly lynched flesh. In both cases, defining ourselves solely by our oppression denies us the very magic of who we are. My feminism simply refuses to give sexism or racism that much power.

Holding on to that protective mantle of victimization requires a hypocrisy and self-censorship I'm no longer willing to give. Calling rappers out for their sexism without mentioning the complicity of the 100 or so video-hos that turned up—G-string in hand—for the shoot; or defending women's reproductive rights without examining the very complicated issue of *male choice*

—specifically the inherent unfairness in denying men the right to choose whether or not *they want* to parent; or discussing the physical and emotional damage of sexism without examining the utterly foul and unloving ways black women treat each other ultimately means fronting like the shit brothers have with them is any less complex, difficult, or painful than the shit we have with ourselves. I am down, however, for a feminism that demands we assume responsibility for our lives.

In my quest to find a functional feminism for myself and my sistas—one that seeks empowerment on spiritual, material, physical, and emotional levels—I draw heavily on the cultural movement that defines my generation. As post–Civil Rights, post-feminist, post-soul children of hip-hop we have a dire need for the truth.

We have little faith in inherited illusions and idealism. We are the first generation to grow up with all the benefits of Civil Rights (i.e., Affirmative Action, government-subsidized educational and social programs) and the first to lose them. The first to have the devastation of AIDS, crack, and black-on-black violence makes it feel like a blessing to reach twenty-five. Love no longer presents itself wrapped in the romance of basement blue lights, lifetime commitments, or the sweet harmonies of The Stylistics and The Chi-Lites.

Love for us is raw like sushi, served up on sex platters from R. Kelly and Jodeci. Even our existences can't be defined in the past's simple terms: house nigga vs. field nigga, ghetto vs. bourgie, BAP vs. boho because our lives are usually some complicated combination of all of the above.

More than any other generation before us, we need a feminism committed to "keeping it real." We need a voice like our music—one that samples and layers many voices, injects its sensibilities into the old and flips it into something new, provocative, and powerful. And one whose occasional hypocrisy, contradictions, and trifeness guarantee us at least a few trips to the terror-dome, forcing us to finally confront what we'd all rather hide from.

We need a feminism that possesses the same fundamental understanding held by any true student of hiphop. Truth can't be found in the voice of any one rapper but in the juxtaposition of many. The keys that unlock the riches of contemporary black female identity lie not in choosing Latifah over Lil' Kim, or even Foxy Brown over Salt-N-Pepa. They lie at the magical intersection where those contrary voices meet—the juncture where "truth" is no longer black and white but subtle, intriguing shades of gray.

from fly-girls
to bitches and hos

F eminist criticism, like many other forms of social analysis, is widely considered part of a hostile white culture. For a black feminist to chastise misogyny in rap publicly would be viewed as divisive and counterproductive. There is a widespread perception in the black community that public criticism of black men constitutes collaborating with a racist society. . . .

> Michele Wallace, "When Black Feminism
> Faces the Music, and the Music Is Rap"
> The New York Times[1]

Lord knows our love jones for hip-hop is understandable. Props given to rap music's artistic merits, its irrefutable impact on pop culture, its ability to be alternately beautiful, poignant, powerful, strong, irreverent, visceral, and mesmerizing—homeboy's clearly got it like that. But in between the beats, booty shaking, and hedonistic abandon, I have to wonder if there isn't something inherently unfeminist in supporting a music that repeatedly reduces me to tits and ass and encourages pimping on the regular. While it's human to occasionally fall deep into the love thang with people or situations that simply aren't good for you, feminism alerted me long ago to the dangers of romancing a misogynist (and ridiculously fine, brilliant ones with gangsta leans are no exception). Perhaps the nonbelievers were right, maybe what I'd been mistaking for love and commitment for the last twenty years was really nothing but a self-destructive obsession that made a mockery of my feminism.

I needed to know, once and for all, if it was in the best interests of me and my sistas to stay in what was—admittedly—a strange and often painful relationship. The time had come for a little heart-to-heart, so I started by writing my homeboy this letter:

You know, Boo,

It's been six years since I've been writing about hip-hop on the womanist tip and I'm still getting asked the same questions. At work, the intelligentsia types want to know if "Given the undeniably high content of sexism and misogyny in rap music, isn't a declared commitment to both, well, incongruous?" And my girls, they just come right out, " You still wit that nigga?"

So I tell them how good you do that thing you do. Laugh and say I'm just a slave to your rhythms. Then I wax poetic about your artistic brilliance and the voice (albeit predominantly male) you give an embattled, pained nation. And then I assure them that I call you out on all of your sexism on the regular. That works until someone, usually a sista-friend, calls me out and says that while all of that was valid, none of it explains why I stayed in an obviously abusive relationship. And I can't lie, Boo, that would stress me. 'Cuz my answers would start sounding like those battered women I write about.

Sure, I'd say (all defensive). It's easy to judge—to wonder what any woman in her right mind would be doing with that wack motherfucka if you're entering now, before the sweet times. But the sweetness was there in the beginning of this on-again, off-again love affair. It started almost twenty years ago, around the time when Tony Boyd all mocked-neck and fine gave me my first tongue kiss in the back of I.S. 148 and the South Bronx gave birth to a culture.

The old-school deejays and M.C.'s performed community service at those schoolyard jams. Intoxicating the crowd with beats and rhymes, they were like shamans sent to provide us with temporary relief from the ghetto's blues. As for sistas, we donned our flare-leg Lees and medallions, became fly-girls, and gave up the love. Nobody even talked about sexism in hip-hop back in the day. All an M.C. wanted then was to be the baddest in battle, have a fly-girl, and take rides in his fresh O.J. If we were being objectified (and I guess we were) nobody cared. At the time, there seemed to be greater sins than being called "ladies" as in "All the ladies in the house, say, Oww!"

Or "fly-girls" as in "what you gonna do?" Perhaps it was because we were being acknowledged as a complementary part of a whole.

But girlfriend's got a point, Boo. We haven't been fly-girls for a very long time. And all the love in the world does not erase the stinging impact of the new invectives and brutal imagery—ugly imprints left on cheeks that have turned the other way too many times. The abuse is undeniable. Dre, Short, Snoop, Scarface, I give them all their due but the mid school's increasing use of violence, straight-up selfish individualism, and woman-hating (half of them act like it wasn't a woman who clothed and fed their black asses—and I don't care if Mama was Crackhead Annie, then there was probably a grandmother who kept them alive) masks the essence of what I fell in love with even from my own eyes.

Things were easier when your only enemies were white racism and middle-class black folk who didn't want all that jungle music reminding them they had kinky roots. Now your anger is turned inward. And I've spent too much time in the crossfire, trying to explain why you find it necessary to hurt even those who look like you. Not to mention a habit called commercialism and multiple performance failures and I got to tell you, at times I've found myself scrounging for reasons to stay. Something more than twenty years being a long-ass time, and not quite knowing how to walk away from a nigga whose growth process has helped define your existence.

So here I am, Boo, lovin' you, myself, my sistas, my brothers with loyalties that are as fierce as they are divided. One thing I know for certain is that if you really are who I believe you to be, the voice of a nation, in pain and insane, then any thinking black woman's relationship with you is going to be as complicated as her love for black men.

*Whether I like it or not, you play a critical part in defining
my feminism. Only you can give me the answer to the
question so many of us are afraid to ask, "How did we go
from fly-girls to bitches and hos in our brothers' eyes?"*

*You are my key to the locker room. And while it's true
that your music holds some of fifteen- to thirty-year-old
black men's ugliest thoughts about me, it is the only place
where I can challenge them. You are also the mirror in which
we can see ourselves. And there's nothing like spending time
in the locker room to bring sistas face-to-face with the ways
we straight-up play ourselves. Those are flesh-and-blood
women who put their titties on the glass. Real-life ones who
make their livings by waiting backstage and slingin' price
tags on the punanny. And if our feminism is ever going to
mean anything, theirs are the lives you can help us to save.
As for the abuse, the process is painful, yes, but wars are not
won by soldiers who are afraid to go to the battleground.*

*So, Boo, I've finally got an answer to everybody that
wants to talk about the incongruity of our relationship.
Hip-hop and my feminism are not at war but my community
is. And you are critical to our survival.*

I'm yours, Boo. From cradle to the grave.

I guess it all depends on how you define the f-word.
My feminism places the welfare of black women and

the black community on its list of priorities. It also maintains that black-on-black love is essential to the survival of both.

We have come to a point in our history, however, when black-on-black love—a love that's survived slavery, lynching, segregation, poverty, and racism—is in serious danger. The stats usher in this reality like taps before the death march: According to the U.S. Census Bureau, the number of black two-parent households has decreased from 74 percent to 48 percent since 1960. The leading cause of death among black men ages fifteen to twenty-four is homicide. The majority of them will die at the hands of other black men.[2]

Women are the unsung victims of black-on-black crime. A while back, a friend of mine, a single mother of a newborn (her "babyfather"—a brother—abdicated responsibility before their child was born) was attacked by a pit bull while walking her dog in the park. The owner (a brother) trained the animal to prey on other dogs and the flesh of his fellow community members.

A few weeks later my moms called, upset, to tell me about the murder of a family friend. She was a troubled young woman with a history of substance abuse, aggravated by her son's murder two years ago.

She was found beaten and burned beyond recognition. Her murderers were not "skinheads," "The Man," or "the racist white power structure." More likely than not, they were brown men whose faces resembled her own.

Clearly, we are having a very difficult time loving one another.

Any feminism that fails to acknowledge that black folks in nineties America are living and trying to love in a war zone is useless to our struggle against sexism. Though it's often portrayed as part of the problem, rap music is essential to that struggle because it takes us straight to the battlefield.

My decision to expose myself to the sexism of Dr. Dre, Ice Cube, Snoop Dogg, or the Notorious B.I.G. is really my plea to my brothers to tell me who they are. I need to know why they are so angry at me. Why is disrespecting me one of the few things that make them feel like men? What's the haps, what are you going through on the daily that's got you acting so foul?

As a black woman and a feminist I listen to the music with a willingness to see past the machismo in order to be clear about what I'm *really* dealing with. What I hear frightens me. On booming track after booming track, I hear brothers talking about spending each day high as hell on malt liquor and Chronic. Don't sleep. What passes for "40 and a blunt" good times in most of hip-hop is really alcoholism, substance abuse, and chemical dependency. When brothers can talk so cavalierly about killing each other and then reveal that they have no expectation to see their twenty-first birthday, that is straight-up depression *masquerading* as machismo.

Anyone curious about the processes and pathologies that form the psyche of the young, black, and criminal-minded needs to revisit our dearly departed Notorious B.I.G.'s first album, *Ready to Die*. Chronicling the life and times of the urban "soldier," the album is a blues-laden soul train that took us on a hustler's life journey. We boarded with the story of his birth, strategically stopped to view his dysfunctional, warring family, his first robbery, his first stint in jail, murder, drug-dealing, getting paid, partying, sexin', rappin', mayhem, and death. Biggie's player persona might have momentarily convinced the listener that he was livin' phat without a care in the world but other moments divulged his inner hell. The chorus of "Everyday Struggle": *I don't wanna live no more / Sometimes I see death knockin' at my front door* revealed that "Big Poppa" was also plagued with guilt, regret, and depression. The album ultimately ended with his suicide.

The seemingly impenetrable wall of sexism in rap music is really the complex mask African-Americans often wear both to hide and express the pain. At the close of this millennium, hip-hop is still one of the few forums in which young black men, even surreptitiously, are allowed to express their pain.

When it comes to the struggle against sexism and our intimate relationships with black men, some of the most on-point feminist advice I've received comes from sistas like my mother, who wouldn't dream of using the term. During our battle to resolve our complicated relationships with my equally wonderful and errant father, my mother presented me with the following gems of wisdom, "One of the most important lessons you will ever learn in life and love, is that you've got to love people for what they are—not for who you would like them to be."

This is crystal clear to me when I'm listening to hip-hop. Yeah, sistas are hurt when we hear brothers calling us bitches and hos. But the real crime isn't the name-calling, it's their failure to love us—to be our brothers in the way that we commit ourselves to being their sistas. But recognize: Any man who doesn't truly love himself is incapable of loving us in the healthy way we need to be loved. It's extremely telling that men who can only see us as "bitches" and "hos" refer to themselves only as "niggas."

In the interest of our emotional health and overall sanity, black women have got to learn to love brothers realistically, and that means differentiating between who they are and who we'd like them to be. Black men are engaged in a war where the real enemies—racism and the white power structure—are masters of camou-flage. They've conditioned our men to believe the enemy is brown. The effects of this have been as wicked as they've been debilitating. Being in battle with an enemy that looks just like you makes it hard to believe in the basics every human being needs. For too many black men there is no trust, no community, no family. Just self.

Since hip-hop is the mirror in which so many broth-ers see themselves, it's significant that one of the mu-sic's most prevalent mythologies is that black boys rarely grow into men. Instead, they remain perpetually post-adolescent or die. For all the machismo and testos-terone in the music, it's frighteningly clear that many brothers see themselves as powerless when it comes to facing the evils of the larger society, accepting responsi-bility for their lives, or the lives of their children.

So, sista friends, we gotta do what any rational,

survivalist-minded person would do after finding her-self in a relationship with someone whose pain makes him abusive. We've gotta continue to give up the love but *from a distance that's safe*. Emotional distance is a great enabler of unconditional love and support because it allows us to recognize that the attack, the "bitch, ho" bullshit—isn't personal but part of the illness.

And the focus of black feminists has got to change. We can't afford to keep expending energy on banal discussions of sexism in rap when sexism is only part of a huge set of problems. Continuing on our previous path is akin to demanding that a fiending, broke crack-head not rob you blind because it's *wrong* to do so.

If feminism intends to have any relevance in the lives of the majority of black women, if it intends to move past theory and become functional it has to rescue itself from the ivory towers of academia. Like it or not, hip-hop is not only the dominion of the young, black, and male, it is also the world in which young black women live and survive. A functional game plan for us, one that is going to be as helpful to Shequanna on 142nd as it is to Samantha at Sarah Lawrence, has to recognize hip-hop's ability to articulate the pain our *community* is in and use that knowledge to create a redemptive, healing space.

Notice the emphasis on "community." Hip-hop isn't only instrumental in exposing black men's pain, it brings the healing sistas need right to the surface. Sad as it may be, it's time to stop ignoring the fact that rappers meet "bitches" and "hos" daily—women who reaffirm their depiction of us on vinyl. Backstage, the road, and the 'hood are populated with women who would do anything to be with a rapper sexually for an hour if not a night. It's time to stop fronting like we don't know who rapper Jeru the Damaja was talking about when he said:

> *Now a queen's a queen but a stunt's a stunt*
> *You can tell whose who by the things they want*

Sex has long been the bartering chip that women use to gain protection, material wealth, and the vicarious benefits of power. In the black community, where women are given less access to all of the above, "trickin' " becomes a means of leveling the playing field. Denying the justifiable anger of rappers—men who couldn't get the time of day from these women before a few dollars and a record deal—isn't empowering or strategic. Turning a blind eye and scampering for moral high ground diverts our attention away from the young women who are being denied access to power and are suffering for it.

It might've been more convenient to direct our sista-fied rage attention to "the sexist representation of women" in those now infamous Sir Mix-A-Lot videos, to fuss over *one* sexist rapper, but wouldn't it have been more productive to address the failing self-esteem of the 150 or so half-naked young women who were will-ing, unpaid participants? And what about how flip we are when it comes to using the b-word to describe each other? At some point we've all been the recipients of competitive, unsisterly, "bitchiness," particularly when vying for male attention.

Since being black and a woman makes me fluent in both isms, I sometimes use racism as an illuminating analogy. Black folks have finally gotten to the point where we recognize that we sometimes engage in op-pressive behaviors that white folks have little to do with. Complexion prejudices and classism are illnesses which have their *roots* in white racism but the perpetra-tors are certainly black.

Similarly, sistas have to confront the ways we're com-plicit in our own oppression. Sad to say it, but many of the ways in which men exploit our images and sexuality in hip-hop is done with our permission and cooperation. We need to be as accountable to each other as we believe "race traitors" (i.e., 100 or so brothers in blackface cooning in a skinhead's music video) should be to our community. To acknowledge this doesn't deny our victimization but it does raise the critical issue of whose responsibility it is to end our oppression. As a feminist, I believe it is too great a responsibility to leave to men.

A few years ago, on an airplane making its way to Montego Bay, I received another gem of girlfriend wisdom from a sixty-year-old self-declared non-feminist. She was meeting her husband to celebrate her thirty-fifth wedding anniversary. After telling her I was twenty-seven and very much single, she looked at me and shook her head sadly. "I feel sorry for your generation. You don't know how to have relationships, especially the women." Curious, I asked her why she thought this was. "The women of your generation, you want to be right. The women of my generation, we didn't care about being right. We just wanted to win."

Too much of the discussion regarding sexism and the music focuses on being right. We feel we're *right* and the rappers are wrong. The rappers feel it's their *right* to describe their "reality" in any way they see fit. The store owners feel it's their *right* to sell whatever the consumer wants to buy. The consumer feels it's his *right* to be able to decide what he wants to listen to. We may be the "rightest" of the bunch but we sure as hell ain't doing the winning.

I believe hip-hop can help us win. Let's start by recognizing that its illuminating, informative narration and its incredible ability to articulate our collective pain is an invaluable tool when examining gender relations. The information we amass can help create a redemptive, healing space for brothers and sistas.

We're all winners when a space exists for brothers to honestly state and explore the roots of their pain and subsequently their misogyny, sans judgment. It is criminal that the only space our society provided for the late Tupac Shakur to examine the pain, confusion, drug addiction, and fear that led to his arrest and his eventual assassination was in a prison cell. How can we win if a prison cell is the only space an immensely talented but troubled young black man could dare utter these words: "Even though I'm not guilty of the charges they gave me, I'm not innocent in terms of the way I was acting. I'm just as guilty for not doing things. Not with this case but with my life. I had a job to do and I never showed up. I was so scared of this responsibility that I was running away from it."[3] We have to do better than this for our men.

And we have to do better for ourselves. We desperately need a space to lovingly address the uncomfortable issues of our failing self-esteem, the ways we sexualize and objectify ourselves, our confusion about sex and love and the unhealthy, unloving, unsisterly ways we treat each other. Commitment to developing these spaces gives our community the potential for remedies based on honest, clear diagnoses.

As I'm a black woman, I am aware that this doubles my workload—that I am definitely going to have to listen to a lot of shit I won't like—but without these candid discussions, there is little to no hope of exorcising the illness that hurts and sometimes kills us.

strongblackwomen

To Whom it May Concern:

For reasons of emotional health and overall sanity, I've retired from being a STRONGBLACKWOMAN. Since I've been acting like a SBW for most of my life, I've taken the liberty of drafting a re-orientation memo.

To the white folks I work with——the fake "Fine" and compulsory smile? Gone. Deaded. Don't look for it. From now on, when asked "How are you?" I'm going to tell you the truth ——so if you really don't give a shit, do yourself a favor and don't ask. Some days I really am an evil black woman.

To the folks in my life who are used to calling me at all hours of the A.M. or P.M. and repeatedly dumping their emotional refuse —start looking for a therapist. I apologize for not telling you before that I'm not the "strongest sista" you know, that my shit is not "always so damn together." (Then again you would have known if you'd interjected an occasional, "Hey, girl, how you doing?" in your tirades.) There are days my shit is downright raggedy and on those days I'm not feeling you. I've officially given myself permission to ignore all twenty of your messages on my machine, especially the ones telling me you feel abandoned.

To the brothers trying to kick it. Stop. Let me save you some time. If my financial independence, education, ambition, looks, or basic determination to survive makes you question whether or not you'd have anything to give a such STRONG-BLACKWOMAN, don't bother. Return to the valley of the chickenheads, cuz I don't fuck wit' that anymore. SBWs do not have needs. I got plenty—and I'll gladly tell them to you while I'm running your bathwater, or you're rubbing me down with oil, or we're playing tag with our tongues. Bring it on if and only if you really believe you deserve me.

And while I'm at it, mad love for my peeps who didn't need anything of this, who knew I was never a STRONG-BLACKWOMAN—just fronting. Thanks for sticking around while I was tripping. Y'all know shit goes. We get there in the by and by.

Peace & Love,

Joan

Since sistas are quick to call themselves STRONGBLACKWOMEN and loathe to call themselves feminists, I realize my retirement requires explanation. This is not to be confused with being strong, black, and a woman. I'm still alla that. I draw strength daily from the history of struggle and survival that is a black woman's spiritual legacy. What I kicked to the curb was the years of social conditioning that told me it was my destiny to live my life as BLACKSUPER-WOMAN Emeritus. That by the sole virtues of my race and gender I was supposed to be the consummate professional, handle any life crisis, be the dependable rock for every soul who needed me, and, yes, the classic—require less from my lovers than they did from me because after all, I was a STRONGBLACK-WOMAN and they were just ENDANGEREDBLACK-MEN.

Retirement was ultimately an act of salvation. Being an SBW was killing me slowly. Cutting off my air supply.

It started one autumn, when I no longer noticed the changing of the leaves. Fall came and went without my usual marveling at nature's decision to appear most beautiful before she dies—adorning herself in brilliant burgundies, oranges, and golds. Part of it was work. My job as a staff writer for a new black entertainment magazine kept me too busy for anything that wasn't industry related—including, pathetically enough, family and friends—and often at the expense of my emotional and physical well-being. But after paying the hellish dues expected of a Non-Trust-Fund-Having-Writer-Living-in-New-York, I convinced myself this was my dream job. So despite glaring indications that celebrity journalism was rarely made of the stuff that made my nipples hard, I wrote my ass off, stayed fabulous, and sank, deeper and deeper into denial.

Then one night at a record release party for Wu-Tang Clan, the natives got restless. The group's performance was seriously delayed in a venue that was hot, funky, and filled way past capacity. Damage was minimal—a bumrushed V.I.P. area and a few fights, broken tables, and chairs. As a vet of live hip-hop performances, I tend not to spook easily, but that night the familiar anger and testosterone left me inexplicably fearful and gasping for air. Panicked, I broke out sans keys, wallet, or good-byes to homegirls.

I tried to write the incident off to a long-overdue aversion to concert crowds, but the feeling that high-tailed me out the club that night followed me. It found me in elevators, cars, even rooms without open windows. Soon it was clear that claustrophobia was stalking me and about 80 percent of the time it was kicking my ass.

Then came the tears. The first ones felt foreign, like the forgotten reflex of an activity abandoned long ago, a ritual I'd re-evaluated and determined useless somewhere along the line. I rarely shed tears for myself in those days. Not only because I was an invulnerablesuperdiva incapable of pain (although there was much of that in the mix), but the endless masking I did from one day to the next was so convincing, I feared becoming confused. It is an unnatural act for masks to cry.

The sentence that started the initial downpour fell from the lips of a very brown and beautiful man whom I'd kissed deeply, passionately, and a bit too quickly. "Your fragility scares me." But that did not scare him as much as my determination to deny it, even to myself. "Your pain is so real," he whispered shakily. "I can feel it. It's so deep it would consume both of us." Then gathering strength but not volume he gave me his decision. "Let me love you as your friend."

It was, of course, the prelude to good-bye.

The fact that the brother was dead-on hardly made

me feel better. I was tired and miserable most of the time. But each time I'd try admitting this the SBW inside would launch a fuckin' tirade. *Girl, what more do you want. You got a good job, a fly-ass apartment, and a work/social calendar most niggas would kill for. Stop bitching and handle it.* I'd internalized the SBW credo: No matter how bad shit gets, handle it alone, quietly, and with dignity. The truth was, much of what was going on in my life shouldn't have been handled silently or stoically by anybody.

Friends and family were of little help because I refused to let them in. I didn't know how. Like most SBWs, I'd developed a real fear of vulnerability or imperfection. The few times I tried, it seemed like I could I barely get the words out before somebody reminded me I was a STRONGBLACKWOMAN. So I listened to the SBW in me and retreated in angry silence. I told no one that my highly dysfunctional relationship with my father was wreaking havoc on my self-esteem and relationships with men. I swallowed the constant rage I felt at the paucity of black editors at what was supposed to be a black magazine. I helped my crimey of damn near two decades with wedding preparations while I mourned what felt like the loss of my best friend. And nightly I was plagued by that absence of air, because I'd fall asleep drowning in tears.

Finally, in a fit of desperation I went to see my godmother.

Iconic of the sistas of her time, Iya is an eclectic blend of black girl sass and sagacity with forties glam, fifties traditionalism, and all the hell-raising rebellion of the sixties and seventies. She's also intensely spiritual, brutally blunt, and has a perceptiveness that borders on psychic. I've come to depend on it—greatly. I told her as much as I could. (Everything except the claustrophobia. That shit sounded crazy, even to me.)

"So your world is starting to close in on you, hmm?" she asked, responding to the details of my latest troubles. Then, puffing on her cigarette with a Hepburnian fierceness, she told me an old Yoruba fable.

There once was this marvelous singing bird who lived in a splendiferous castle. The king was so taken with the bird's beauty that he built it a magnificent cage with all the amenities a bird's heart could possibly desire. Much to the king's dismay, however, the bird fell into silent sadness—never singing nor preening itself—and languished in a general state of despair.

Soon the king started to fear for the bird's life, so

he went to see his godfather. He told him to put the bird on a very long leash and allow it to fly farther and farther afield each day. The bird would make long outings each day and seemed to be doing much better.

One day the bird did not return from its daily outing. Concerned, the king followed the long leash. He traveled past the beautiful castle and the lush forest for a very long time, until the landscape became quite parched and unattractive. In the midst of this, however, he heard a bird singing the most melodious song he'd ever heard. He looked up, and to his utter amazement there was his bird sitting on a scrawny, gnarled, and leafless twig just as joyous and beautiful as she could be.

And it was on that old ugly twig that the bird found its happiness and lived blissfully ever after.

"Oh, by the way," she added casually. "Don't worry about the claustrophobia. It tends to go hand in hand with this type of thing."

I'd learned a long time ago that "How did you know?" was a silly question to ask of a woman who had regular chats with gods and spirits. Instead, I just sighed. "What do you think I should do about it?"

"Well," she said. "I think you better go find yourself that twig."

So one day, in a moment between the airport in Frisco and the flight back to New York, I decided my life—my ability to breathe, let alone write—depended on me leaving New York as quickly as possible. I would spend the winter in San Francisco.

In Frisco I did a few wonderful things. I fell apart regularly in the arms of two deliciously brown men (one a lover, both friends) who faithfully administered the regular doses of TLC I needed to breathe again— unafraid of my tears or fragility. I wrote. Spent lots of time near the water. Heard Oshun's laughter twinkling like bells, urging me to recapture the feminine and discover the fierceness of a black girl's magic. I did and had what I now know to be a powerfully feminist time. Back then though, I was just saving my life.

Perhaps nothing could have saved me from becoming a SBW. Certainly there was a wealth of Women's Studies courses, and an abundance of my foremothers— Michele Wallace, Paula Giddings, and bell hooks, to name a few—scholarly research that tried. In fact, the ultimate anti-SBW manifesto, Wallace's *Black Macho and the Myth of the Superwoman,* was displayed prominently in my study for years. Even though I considered the book a bible for generations of black girls raised to believe the only appropriate response to adversity is to flex like Harriet Tubman, I still managed not to get it. Much to my detriment, I ignored her incisive warning: "For every woman like Harriet Tubman there were twenty who died in childbirth, went mad, or became old by the time they were thirty. The existence of a Harriet Tubman only meant that some unusually talented women had emerged despite a vicious and cruel system of human devastation." [1]

Perhaps the image of my mother at my age, with blood clotting in her lungs, trying desperately to immerse herself in an activity as normal as plaiting her hair before she was rushed off to the hospital, is too viscerally implanted in my childhood memory. Perhaps it's the thought of her pushing my tiny hands away as I made attempts to help her. Perhaps it's because I can't remember my mother ever being afraid unless something threatened her children's well-being.

I am sure it is because I am a black girl and we are a people ruled by Myth. It was once the way we made sense of our world—how we explained the birthing and dying of things and everything that came between. But all of that changed once we were stolen. Myth became white folks' way of making sense of us and the perversions of their institutions. According to their Myth slavery was an act of benevolence bestowed on ungodly savages and primitives. And to those who knew and cared little about us or our prior histories, we became Mammies, Pickaninnies, and Sambos (creatures too simple to survive without a master's guidance), or oversexed, criminal, dangerous Niggers. The latter, of course, possessing a nature that justified every act of barbarism it took to keep them in line.

This was the Myth of the New Place. It was repeated like a mantra whenever the dying breath of black boys fertilized poplar trees; whenever whips set fire to the backs of women carrying seeds unwanted.

It was in this dangerous climate of myth-making that the war to shape black women's identity was waged. We've been fighting it ever since. Their Myth vs. ours. The problem is we've been fighting so long we sometimes forget which Myth belonged to whom.

So here's a reminder about the original SBW. The STRONGBLACKWOMAN was born in the antebellum South. She had a white step-sister named SOUTH-ERNBELLE. Now the effects of revisionist history being what they are, the two are now permanently estranged, but they were once so close their existences depended on each other. Both sisters were the bastard children of racism, sexism, and the white male Myth-makers need for absolute dominance.

The antebellum South was a lousy place to be a woman—black or white. White women fared better than their shackled (and for that matter unshackled) counterparts but their lot still left much to be desired. The price for that mint-julep-sipping-lady-of-leisure status was high. The image of the evil, domineering plantation mistress looms so dominantly in our minds we forget the SB had to surrender all authority to her husband. Giddings breaks it down in *Where and When I Enter.*

> White Southern women found themselves enmeshed in an interracial web in which wives, children, and slaves were *all* expected to obey the patriarchal head of the household. The compliance of White women became inextricably linked to that of the slaves. It was believed that "any tendency of one member of the system to assert themselves against the master threatened the whole." It was often asserted by slavery apologists that any change in the role of women *or* blacks would contribute to [the] downfall of not only slavery but the family and society as well.[2]

Since white men also believed white women were too fragile for thoughts beyond beauty and motherhood, the SOUTHERNBELLE was considered too "virtuous" and "pure" to be sullied with anything as nasty as independent sexual desire. So her myth-making husband assigned her a figurative chastity belt to which he had the only key. She was expected, however, to turn a blind eye to his illicit sexual liaisons with her darker step-sister. It was understood that satisfying her husband's baser needs was not in her nature—that filthy task was best left to black women whose "hot-blooded" constitutions rendered them STRONG enough to take it. So while the SB was "hoisted on a pedestal so high that she was beyond the sensual reach of her own husband, Black women were consigned to the other end of the scale, as mistresses, whores and breeders." [3]

With both racism and sexism pushing it along, the myth that black women were stronger than white women and nastier to boot, permeated the social climate—from the good ol' homestead to Ivy League colleges. Harvard today has one of the most distinguished African-American Studies departments around, but check out Giddings's analysis of Philip A. Bruce's thesis, which was published in 1889.

[Black women] were "morally obtuse" and "openly licentious," he wrote. But because they were women, their regression was seen as much worse than that of men. For it was women who were "responsible" for molding the institution of marriage and a wholesome family life, which was the "safeguard against promiscuity." In Bruce's eyes, Black women who saw no "immorality in doing what nature prompts," who did not "foster charity" among their own daughters were not only responsible for their own denigration but for that of the *entire race*. Even the Black man's alleged impulse to rape was the Black woman's fault. Historically, the stereotype of the sexually potent Black male was largely based on that of the promiscuous Black female. He would have to be potent, the thinking went, to satisfy such hot-natured women. . . .[4]

Before long the black woman's mythic "strength" became a convenient justification for every atrocity committed on her. It was the Myth-makers rationale, for rape and breeding (and by extension, the lynching of black men)—acts, interestingly enough, that no civilized white man would dream of doing to the STRONGBLACKWOMAN's exalted step-sister, Miss SOUTHERNBELLE.

"Every tenet of the mythology about [the black woman] was used to reinforce the spinelessness and unreliability of the black man, as well as the frivolity and vulnerability of the white woman," explains Wallace. "It was at this point that the black woman gained her reputation for invulnerability. She was key to the labor supply. No one wished to admit that she felt as any woman might about the losses of her children, or that she had any particular attachment to her husband, since he might also have to be sold. . . . She was believed to be not only emotionally callous but physically invulnerable—stronger than [any] white woman and the physical equal of any man of her race. She was stronger than white women in order to justify her performing a kind of labor most white women were now presumed to be incapable of. She was labeled sexually promiscuous because it was imperative that her womb supply the labor force. . . ." [5]

Still, the question remains, if the original STRONG-BLACKWOMAN was really the creation of some fucked-up slave owners, why do contemporary SBWs flaunt the identity like a badge of honor? The answers lie in the complex amalgamation of myths that still surround black female identity. Some of them are unquestionably the racist creations of white folks. Quite a few of them were given to us by our brothers. The rest we gave ourselves.

Wallace catalogs the stereotypes: *Sapphire. Mammy. Workhorse. . . . Always had more opportunities than the black man because she was no threat to the white man so he made it easier for her. Frequently ends up on welfare . . . more educated and makes more money than the black man . . . provides the main support for the family. Not beautiful rather hard looking unless she has white blood, but then very beautiful. The black ones are exotic though, great in bed, tigers. And very fertile . . . She is unsupporting of black men, domineering, castrating. She tends to wear the pants around her house. Very strong . . . tough, unfeminine. Opposed to women's rights movements . . . considers herself already liberated . . . definitely not a dreamer, rigid, inflexible, uncompassionate . . .*[6]

Add the following nineties manifestations to Wallace's mix: *Ghetto Bitch. Project Ho. Welfare Queen. Goldigger. Skeezer. Babymother. Hoochie Mama. Chickenhead. Ball-buster. Too independent. Don't need no man. Waiting to Exhale. Earth. Nubian Queen. The ultimate mother. Selfless and all-sacrificing. Gets up every time she's knocked down. Claire Huxtable—Mother of five. Shenequa—a decade younger than Claire and Mother of six. Loud as hell. Silent and suffering. Not whiny, like a white girl. Paid, paid, paid. Poor, poor, poor.*

"From this intricate web of mythology which surrounds the black woman a fundamental image emerges," concludes Wallace. "It is of a woman of inordinate strength, with an ability for tolerating an unusual amount of misery and heavy distasteful work. This woman does not have the same fears, weaknesses, and insecurities as other women, but believes herself to be and is, in fact, stronger emotionally than most men. Less of a woman in that she is the embodiment of Mother Earth, the quintessential mother with infinite sexual, life-giving, and nurturing reserves. In other words she is a Superwoman." [7]

The original SBW and her alleged "super strength" was a myth created by whites to rationalize their brutality. The contemporary SBW, however, is *our* internalization of this mythology. Superhuman strength was the salvageable shred of dignity remaining after sexism and racism ravaged our images. In turn, we fabricated an identity out of it. Becoming SBWs was the emotional inoculation needed to protect us from the Mythmakers' lies.

There are inherent dangers, however, in building an identity based on the prejudices of one's oppressor. Eventually the line between Myth and Mortality becomes dangerously, irreversibly blurred.

Hip-hop's fallen heroes provide a haunting example. The music's greatest gift and its heaviest burden is its legacy of urban mythology. Hip-hop will always be remembered as that bittersweet moment when young black men captured the ears of America and defined themselves on their own terms. Regenerating themselves as seemingly invincible bass gods, gangsta griots, and rhythm warriors, they turned a defiant middle finger to a history that racistly ignored or misrepresented them.

And we loved them for it. Selfishly we chose to ignore the dangers of rappers believing their own myths. Instead of reminding them of their mortality, we demanded that they come harder, phatter, and deffer. Sensing our worship was conditional they donned ghetto realness and wore it like armor. Inevitably, we all suffered the consequences. Eazy-E's untimely death from AIDS and Tupac's and Biggie's senseless murders painfully reminded us of our heroes' mortality. At the end of the day we were left with what we'd always known: Young black men are not invincible—they get shot, go to jail, and die all the time.

The harrowing tale of Dianna Green, the sista whose suicide was plastered over the front page of *The Wall Street Journal,* is yet another example. As the senior VP at Duquesne Light Co. and a major Pittsburgh power broker, Green, in the words of *Essence* magazine, was the type of sista we all "looked up to, admired, and tried to learn from." She was "the role model who made the old folks proud and inspired the young ones. The well-connected sister we all want to meet" who "chairs our committees and leads our fund-raising efforts." Green was "the matriarch, the giver who is always out and about, helping, saving, nurturing, protecting, mentoring, loving, encouraging, leading— making sure everybody else's back is covered but her own."

Green, it seems was a STRONGBLACKWOMAN if there ever was one. And in true SBW fashion, she camouflaged her personal pain. Diabetes was causing her eyesight to fail. Her mother and brother died within months of each other. And after years of service to Duquesne, she was fired after the utility company discovered she'd allegedly lied about receiving an MBA on her résumé. Tragically, Green sought the only relief she knew. "Hours after the company issued a polite memo to employees announcing her departure, the superwoman was dead."[8] With a Bible by her side, Green ended her misery with a .22 caliber gun and a single shot to the head.

Green's story brings to light a dichotomy that SBWs grapple with daily. There's no question that the myth of the STRONGBLACKWOMAN empowers us in many ways. When you're raised to believe that the ability to kick adversity's ass is a birthright—a by-product of gender and melanin—you tend to tackle life's afflictions tenaciously. This is a useful quality, no doubt. However, this myth also tricks many of us into believing we can carry the weight of the world.

Truth be told there is much to indicate otherwise. Black women are more likely to die from cancer, AIDS, heart attack, diabetes, high blood pressure, kidney failure, and domestic violence than white women—who outlive us by an average of six years. Between 1986 and 1991, the number of black women in state prisons on drug-related charges alone soared a staggering 828 percent—making us the fastest-growing group in the prison system.[9] Only 56 percent of us are employed full-time (vs. 60 percent of black men). Black-on-black marriages are down to 38 percent. Forty-six percent of us are raising families alone and many of us in poverty —the average income for black women is a paltry $11,956.[10] Black women are not impervious to pain. We're simply adept at *surviving*.

The problem for SBW is telling the difference.

Daily Meditation for SBWs in Recovery
For some reason, we believe struggle is noble. We think it brings us special rewards or that the

God force is pleased with us when we struggle.
Struggling people have so much to say about the
things they are struggling with that they hardly have
time to get anything done. Struggling people know
how to struggle well. They know what to wear,
where to go, and how to behave in a way that will
create struggle. Struggling people impose
conditions, restrictions, and expectations upon
themselves, because it is easier to struggle doing
nothing than it is to bring up and use the creative
force within. Struggling people love to sacrifice in
the name of struggle. They sacrifice themselves,
their families and if you are not careful, they will
sacrifice you.

God does not ask us to struggle. What we are told
is, "Come up to Me all ye that labor and I will give
ye rest"
  —Iyanla Vanzant, *Acts of Faith*

Any SBW that doubts her affinity for struggle needs
to look no further than the standard list of black female
icons. "The Widows"—Coretta Scott King, Myrlie
Evers, Dr. Betty Shabazz—usually head the list, followed by Harriet Tubman and Billie Holiday. It wasn't

until the tragic passing and postmortem praises of Dr. Shabazz that many black folks even realized that her life's accomplishments encompassed more than marrying "Our Shining Black Prince" and surviving the brutality of his murder. Her commitment to education, activism, and family would have made her passing just as tragic a loss for our community if Malcolm had lived to a ripe old age, or if the two had never met at all.

I wonder, though, if we would have paid the same degree of attention. If we woulda granted her the status of heroine if Sista Betty had lived a charmed life, no friendlier with struggle than the rest of us. Because unlike contemporary black male heroes—Colin Powell, Michael Jordan, or Jesse Jackson—being talented, famous, wealthy, and powerful has never quite been enough to clinch black heroine status. Eternal public suffering is a non-negotiable prerequisite.

Recognition for their laudable strengths duly noted, black women's icons rarely have lives any of us would want to live—not really. While little black boys grow up hoping one day to "Be Like Mike" we pray our daughters will never know the darkest depths of depression and substance abuse or the pain of losing men they love to senseless violence. What we hope for daughters and ourselves is if faced with the same degree of adversity as our sheroes we'll emulate their strengths. We remember, on the days we feel like laying down and dying, the list of their accomplishments against ridiculous odds. But do we want be them? No. 'Cuz their existences were simply too damn hard.

Too hard. Even as I write the words that unrepentant SBW voice tells me I'm committing some sort of sacrilege. That there's something wrong with saying *I want to grow up and be like, I don't know, Oprah, 'cuz the sista went through some shit but she's rich and powerful, smart, spiritually balanced, and above all else, pretty damned happy with her life.* Demanding the same sort of privilege afforded white folks and black men—specifically, icons whose lives we'd actually want to live—still feels like an inappropriate desire for women Zora Neale Hurston once described "as the mules of the world."

In all fairness, this seems to be a problem not limited to black women. Once, when trying to come up with a speaker in the entertainment business who seemed to master the art of "having it all"—successful career, kids, hubby, health, wealth, etc.—I suggested actress, singer, ex–Miss America Vanessa Williams. At the

time, she not only possessed all of the above but managed to rise to the top despite a scandal which would
have ruined a lesser soul. She was quickly dismissed as
an inappropriate candidate. "Too beautiful, too perfect," said the multiracial group. "Not enough women
would be able to identify with her." Her life, it seemed,
was simply going too well.

Ironically enough, acknowledging my own addiction
jones came at a time when my life was uncharacteristi-
cally free of drama. Once my peeps noticed the way the
Stinson Beach sunsets, the Mission's perfect burritos, or
the night air perfumed with eucalyptus and jasmine
could make me skip—unencumbered—like a child,
they wasted no time. Northern Cali's many treasures
were laid out like jewels at my feet. And with a good
six-hour drive between me and L.A's entertainment
scene, even work was surprisingly refreshing. But for
every magical moment I experienced, there were
frightening lapses in identity. As an SBW I was well
versed in the art of survival. I knew how to do "tired,"
"stressed," "hanging in there," but "easy?"—I didn't
have the foggiest.

I actually had to learn *how* to put my needs first.
Giving both Guilt and Struggle the finger, I confessed
to the universe I wanted more out of life than simply

being a STRONGBLACKWOMAN. In fact, I wanted every delicious morsel she had to offer me. More important, I wanted to know how to receive it. I wanted what men call "having it all."

But before I could officially become a SBW in recovery, I also had to admit that tenuous grip on sanity I was feeling in New York was *not* caused by the demands of the industry, a bananas schedule, or wack relationships. A great deal of the stress in my life was because I subconsciously *chose* to do shit the hard way. As much as I complained about it, the props I received for "keeping my head up" not only validated my sense of identity, they assuaged the very real wounds that racism and sexism had inflicted on my ego. So instead of acknowledging my mortality—exercising my God-given right to say, "Hold up, enough is enough," I arrogantly said, "Bring it on." And the universe gave me exactly what I asked for.

As racist and sexist in origin as it may be, contemporary black women perpetuate the myth of the SBW for reasons very similar to our antebellum counterparts: It boosts our fractured self-esteems. As the granddaughters of the Civil Rights, Black Power, and Feminist movements, this is a difficult thing to admit. Most of us want to believe that we're finally over some shit—

that our egos are finally immune to daily assaults of racism and sexism—but that's far from the case. We've just learned to suffer on the hush-hush.

So we find ways to battle those oh-so-retro but devilishly persistent voices—the ones that say *Fuck it, I just can't find a way to love my complexion, features, body, hair today, okay, 'cuz society's letting me know by way of callous invisibility that my kinda black beauty just ain't in vogue— and yes, I am attracted to him but threatened by her because of that light skin and good hair. . . . Look at all this fucking garbage/noise/violence in my neighborhood, maybe what the white folks say is true, niggas don't have better 'cuz they don't want better. . . . Yeah, yeah, yeah, I know about all the statistics but yo endangered black ass ain't smelling the pussy unless you gotta job, degree, and a plan. . . . Well, there's a new sista in the immediate proximity—betta watch my job or my man. . . .*

And on the days these voices start gaining ground, STRONG is a helluva consolation prize.

Perhaps one of the most loving things sistas can do for themselves is to erase this tired obligation of super-strength. Instead, let's claim our God/dess-given right to imperfections and vulnerability. As black women it's time to grant ourselves our humanity. My girl Amber-sunshower, singer, songwriter, self-described post-feminist states it eloquently: "Black women deserve to be loved and feel the fulfillment of life on all levels. I am a woman and black, but I'm human first. I am just as loving as my Asian, white, or Latina sisters and need to be treated with just as much sensitivity. My strength is that of all women—to love unconditionally, to bear children, to be connected to the spiritual universe by that divine order."

strong**black**women -n-
endangered**black**men

. . . this is not a love story

All the good black men are not gay, on drugs, or
chasing the skirt tails of white women. Many of them
line Brooklyn streets where dreadlocked dons can be found
flexing dance hall vibes and Hilfiger-wearing Casanovas kick
hip-hop-laced seductions.

All the good black men are not in jail or taken. Their
strong sepia arms can be spotted early in the A.M., picking
up our garbage or conducting the rush hour trains. Their
ivory smiles illuminate evening skies as they peep us tracing
muscle paths from the bottoms of their Nikes well past the

thigh lines of their biker shorts; checking them out as they're shedding their ties and hustling out of office doors. It's not that I was insensitive to all my McMillan-reading sistas who were trying to exhale.

I was, in truth, distracted.

Brooklyn's spring/summer air seemed pregnant with possibilities. . . .

I was over *Waiting to Exhale* shortly after reading the book (tedious) and long before I saw the movie (entertaining). But certain phenomena capture the collective consciousness and render us all accountable. So when folks started touting *Exhale* as the most realistic portrait of black male/female relationships to appear in print/celluloid, every less than catatonic Nubian from Brooklyn to Bonefuck was expected to comment. Even mainstream media wanted to know if it was true. Have black women really given up on black men? Have they really lost the love?

The questions at first seemed somewhat preposterous. This type of cluelessness was to be expected from the mainstream, but black folks? I mean, really. The brothers accusing *Exhale* of "dogging the black male image" were bad enough. (And where were they during the onslaught of the urban black male pathology genre? Or is it okay to make movies where niggas can't do shit besides kill, slang dope, get high, and die as long as they're written and directed by brothers?) But questioning the love?

Please. When it comes to brothers, sistas got love wells that spring eternal. Did they really have to look any further than their own lives to be reminded that no matter how mean, raggedy, funky, or lame a brother gets there'll be some sista out there claiming she's got enough love to fix him? Couldn't they tell from the rallying cries of support we gave Mike Tyson and O. J. Simpson (instead of the women they wounded)? Hadn't they witnessed the dance some of us would gladly do on the next heifer's grave just to keep a man—or steal him? There are clearly times we love them more than each other. Couldn't they see that a sista's "Niggas ain't shit" mentality is usually the scar left to remind her of the time she loved some brother more than herself?

Contrary to the beliefs of many, the phenomenal success of *Exhale* did not demonstrate that black women en masse are acting like racist white folks—too blinded by our prejudices to see black men's intrinsic beauty and worth. Rather it was a clear indication of sistas' justifiable pre-occupation with the rather sorry state of black love in the nineties. It demonstrated that black women are painfully aware of our increasing inability to form lasting healthy, loving relationships and families. Our willingness to look to simplistic theories depicting every brother as a dog and every sista as a biological time bomb waiting to explode for answers, however, reveals that we are absolutely confounded by the causes.

As for the black women who really believe *Waiting to Exhale* was a testimony to the paucity of not only black men, but their overall capacity for goodness (instead of a story about four otherwise intelligent black women, who, when it came to relationships, made some less than wise choices), their response unmasks a well-hidden truth. The men we attract/allow in our lives are reflections of not only who but where we are. Spiritually and emotionally. They're bottom-line reminders of how we feel about ourselves.

In light of this, it's not at all surprising that the sista who swears "all the good black men are taken, gay, on drugs, or in prison" usually kicks off her tirade by affirming her status as a STRONGBLACKWOMAN. SBWs have a tendency to fall hard for their mythological counterparts—ENDANGEREDBLACKMEN.

During slavery, the myth of the STRONGBLACK-WOMAN could only be sustained if brothers were depicted as inherently weaker than not only white men, but also black women. When contemporary black women erroneously internalize these myths we do ourselves and our relationships a grave injustice. 'Cuz it's impossible to embrace even one of racism's lies without becoming hopelessly entangled in a web of others. While black women don't buy into racism's categorical depictions of our men as lazy, stupid, unreliable, or criminally devoid of values, many believe, on some level or another, that the men we love are less capable of surviving the afflictions of life than we are. We sympathetically believe they are not necessarily weak, but ENDANGERED.

Then, armed with beauty shop conspiracy theories grounded in varying degrees of truth, we attribute our pain and loneliness to some cruel numbers game. *Well, you know girl, they're more brothers in jail than in college.* Our frustrations are somewhat justified. There *are* more of us than them (100 to 85 in the 25–44 age group).[1] We *are* more likely to get college degrees, and they are more likely to marry outside the race. However, when you compare the fates that both black men and women suffer at the hands of racism, brothers are really no more of an "endangered species" than we are. Black men suffer (and often die) from violence, imprisonment, drug abuse, and unemployment at rates that are disproportionately higher than their white counterparts, but black women suffer a similar fate when it comes to disease, drug abuse, and domestic violence. Our suffering is just less well documented.

While doing the research for this book (not to mention trying to gain some insight on the less than perfect state of my own relationships), I frequently asked women to share their feelings about black men. The overwhelming consensus of the 100 or so sistas I kicked it with was: Black men have their faults and sistas have their frustrations but the defining emotion is Love. Always Love. The frequency and ease of their answers made me a little suspect. Our relationships with black men seemed far too complex for such a limited emotional repertoire.

So I started to ask about other things. I asked them to talk about respect. Invariably sistas would talk at length about black men's disrespect for us, specifically the myriad ways their sexism has been injurious to our bodies, spirits, and minds. And while the hurt inflicted by sexism is powerful and real, *disrespect* is not what I wanted to talk about. I wanted to talk about black men and Respect—specifically the brothers who lived lives they wanted to emulate, challenged them to become better people, or were instrumental in their growth. Then I asked them to count the black men in their lives they respected. The answers were disturbing. A handful of sisters could recall more than five, but the average hovered around one or two. And when I asked them to name the number they'd been intimate with, the numbers often shot down to zero.

Love without respect is a lethal thing. It is at the

heart of any dysfunctional, abusive relationship. All the unconditional love in the world does not negate the truth. The ENDANGEREDBLACKMAN is a creature black women have learned to love, but he is not one we respect.

And our relationships are suffering from a lack of respect that's as virulent as it is mutual.

For so many black women the process starts with an early heartbreak. We cannot respect what we do not know.

Black America is quickly becoming a nation of fatherless daughters. The hip-hop generation is the product of that one-out-of-two divorce rate.[2] We comprise the two-thirds of black children who are born to single parents. The statistics do not begin to tell our stories —the daughters who've had violence, imprisonment, illness, addiction, depression, or abandonment rob them of fathers—both physically and emotionally.

Is it any wonder, in light of these facts, that so many of us grow up loving but not respecting black men? For most of our lives the folks who put food on the table, clothes on our backs, roofs over our heads, and educated our minds were black women doing it all alone. We were raised to believe that it was the women, not the men, who were the stronger, capable, more responsible ones. They were the ones we could trust and rely on. The men, we learned, were apt to drop the ball.

On our community's crusades to save the "endangered black male" much emphasis has been placed on the necessary role black men play in the rearing of their sons. Black educators advocated nationwide rallies for the development of all-black-male schools in order to provide black boys with appropriate, hands-on role models. Much erroneous ado has been made about single black women's alleged "innate inability" to successfully rear male children. The rearing of girl-children in our community, however, is frequently dismissed as "women's work." Precious little attention is paid to the significant role black men play in shaping their daughters' ideas about themselves and love.

For many black women, the realization only comes in the wake of serial unsuccessful relationships.

Unfortunately, Olufemi's* story is all too common. She is the child of a beautiful, charming woman and an incredibly charismatic and talented man. Since she walks through the world in full possession of both her parents' gifts, her friends are often confused by her

---

* Not her real name.

perpetual relationship dramas. It confuses Olufemi most of all. When the twenty-two-year-old actress finally noticed the undeniable similarities between her father, David Everton,* and her boyfriends, she stopped dating for well over a year.

"My father is a renowned Afri-Caribbean poet and scholar," she explains. "We were really, really close until I turned seven. Then my parents started having problems. My earliest memories of their relationship are pretty fucked-up. The first time I ever saw my mother cry was during my birthday party one year when the mailman delivered my father's divorce request."

Once her father returned to Trinidad, their relationship took a turn for the worse. Olufemi found she had to share him with his many worlds: academics, an active political/social life, and the arts. In time, he remarried, had a new family, and suffered from severe bouts of alcoholism. Olufemi's memories of their relationship during this time are marred by frequent, inexplicably long periods of no communication and many broken promises when it came to visits and finances. What should have been the shared responsibility of raising her was often left solely to her mother.

* Not his real name.

"He was really spread too thin," she recalls sadly. "I mean, as an adult I can attribute certain things to my father's alcoholism, but as a little girl, they were hard to understand."

In order to deal with her hurt and anger, Olufemi tried to numb her emotions and "file them." She dropped out of college, spent a lot of time getting high, and chose men, who, like her father, were charming and talented but troubled, often battling some sort of substance abuse and wholly incapable of commitment. "Totally emotionally abusive," she says. To maintain the relationships she employed the same negative coping mechanisms she'd developed to deal with her father's negligence. "I guess I believed loving them enough would help them change. Basically, I'd convinced myself that having 30 percent of someone was the same as having 90 percent."

Things finally improved for Olufemi and her father when he checked himself into a rehabilitation program. His recovery did much to cement their relationship as friends, but she still has a great deal of difficulty accepting him as a "father." "Like most people, I love David Everton—the man. In fact, I adore him. It's hard not to. He's beautiful, charismatic, and talented." She laughs. "But you definitely have to catch my father as he flows. He just can't be committed to certain things.

And I can accept that from David Everton, the man. But dealing with it from David Everton, my father, is too difficult. His inability to handle certain aspects of his life has caused the people who love him quite a bit of pain."

She still has doubts about her ability to sustain a healthy relationship. She's "come to expect pain from things you love too much."

God. How many times have I been there.

From the ages of four to seven I cried inconsolably each time my father left the house. No one knew quite what to make of this. I was too young to understand the dangers that lurked outside our South Bronx apartment, and because my father did not keep odd, inexplicable hours, my tantrums were dismissed as the unbridled passions of first love. The origins of my separation anxiety remained a mystery to me until years later, when I was twenty-one and trying to deal with my father's final departure from our home. In many ways my father's decision to return to his native Jamaica was one that as an adult I both understood and respected.

My parents' relationship had fallen upon tempestuous times due to economic hardships, illness, and fundamental differences in how they both viewed the world. Returning to Jamaica was more than my father's

spiritual salvation; it gave my mother the distance necessary to close a painful chasm. But hell hath no fury
like a womanchild scorned. The little girl in me was
experiencing a deep sense of anger and betrayal toward
this man who was supposed to love me unconditionally.

Ever since I could remember, my parents' arguments
had been punctuated with my father's threat to leave
and "go back home." I spent my childhood trying to
circumvent that by being the quintessential daddy's girl.
I saved all major acts of rebellion and acting out for
my mother and continued to worship my father—the
elusive, illusory figure I'd created with arduous devo-
tion. I walked away from that experience with a painful
lesson. I'd grown up fearing that the man I loved most
would one day up and step. As a result, I'd written a
protective "I love you but . . ." clause into all my intimate relationships—irrespective of past promises, irrespective of how perfect a man was or tried to be,
because the men who are supposed to love you most
are capable of jumping ship for reasons that have little
or nothing to do with you.

Since daddy's girls are susceptible to patterns, my
childhood fear of abandonment became a self-fulfilling
prophecy in my romantic relationships. As long as I
held on to the anger I was feeling toward my father,

the disgruntled daddy's girl chose my men for me. And because I was a Lolita with a mad Electra complex, that meant ending up with men that were just like my father: incredibly fine, artistic, passionate, charming— souls with occasional hints of genius and serious problems with accountability. It took a few years and some serious emotional bruises before I realized that my adult needs would never be fulfilled until I let go of the anger. Instead of looking for my father in relationships, I had to learn to accept him for the humanly imperfect man he is.

For some of us the patterns are even more lethal. Vicki* remembers saying that she would never tolerate what her mother took from a man. Yet she managed to choose partners who were violent and abusive almost every single time. The thirty-one-year-old bank clerk remembers her deceased father as a loving man. A Korean War veteran who was addicted to heroin, he often suffered from frightening flashbacks and a predilection for violent confrontations. The victim was usually her mother.

It was only after Vicki narrowly escaped a lover who'd held her captive for hours and beaten her badly

* Not her real name.

—occasionally forcing the muzzle of a loaded gun into her mouth—could she recognize her tendency to follow in her parents' footsteps. She shied away from serious relationships for almost five years.

With the help of a therapist, she came to understand that her parents' relationship left her with no role models. "No one ever taught me what I should expect from a man. How men are supposed to treat women. How they should behave was a complete mystery to me." She learned by constructing her own model of a "good man" from the few positive brothers she knew: a professor, her brother, and a few close friends.

When it comes to the responsibilities black men have to their daughters, Vicki does not mince words. "You know, brothers spend so much time talking about teaching their sons about being righteous black men. I just wish they could see that they teach their daughters a helluva lot about black manhood, whether they're around or not. A lot of women put up with unacceptable behavior from men because we're raised to believe that's just the way men are."

I know sometimes in my house (and occasionally on the streets) it must look as if I'm talking to myself. Mostly I'm talking to my unborn women children.

Making surreptitious pacts with them helps to nullify the debilitating, infuriating potency of a simple little phrase like "just the way men are." I promise that they (and I) will never settle for "just the way men are." They will know what a good man should be. Then I say a prayer to whatever goddess will listen.

Teach this frightened daddy's girl to accept strong, loving black arms. Let the unborn women children learn—not from the pain of absence but through example.

Our experience with men we love but do not respect is not limited to our fathers. In his various nineties manifestations we encounter the EBM at numerous junctures in our lives. In hip-hop and the 'hood he's your slangin', bangin' brother—now a self-described "nigga with an attitude" or that weed- and alcohol-addicted cousin. The ones you pray won't be dead or dangerous faces on the evening news—which they very well could be—since men convinced they're not living to see twenty-one tend not to give a shit about their lives or yours.

He's that frustrating lover whose untapped potential will never be reached 'cuz he's given up on his dreams, and taken to quoting statistics instead. His failure to hold a job, get an education, or take care of his kids is everybody's fault—white people, the system, and even you *'Cuz, you know, black women got it easier because "The Man" don't consider y'all threat.*

He's that womanizing athlete, rapper, or Supreme Court judge who cries racism whenever he gets caught confusing sexual abuse with power.

Fortunately, there are countless black men who do what they gotta do—thrive, take care of their families, contribute to their communities and the society at large —despite the odds. ENDANGEREDBLACKMEN, however, are crippled by a deeply entrenched fatalism for which black women must shoulder some of the blame.

Our lovers are also our brothers. They are our mothers' sons—and black women historically have been forced to raise their male children in a climate of fear. This conversation between author Marita Golden and Dr. Joyce Ladner—two black mothers—pretty much sums it up. "Every generation of black women has experienced tremendous anxiety about keeping their men alive. We as women always had to learn to protect our men from white society," says Ladner, remembering growing up in the fifties when a black man, Mack

Parker, was lynched in Mississippi after being accused of raping a white woman. Ladner was fourteen when Emmett Till was murdered.

"When those men were killed, my fear was for my brothers, my uncles. I was a young girl scared for the men in my family. I remember having nightmares that someone would come and take all the men away. Today it's not the Klan in white sheets that's coming, it's more likely to be another black male. Black women are still afraid for their men."

"Each generation of black mothers," responds Golden, "has hoped our sons would indeed become and always be the 'Strong Men' poet Sterling Brown wrote of, who, undaunted and unbowed by racism, 'keep coming, keep coming.' And of our sons, we eternally ask how will they live, will they succeed." [3]

Faced with these daunting realities most black mothers rely heavily on their most abundant resource, unconditional love. And with the absence of so many fathers, more often than not it's a blessing. When that love is tainted with unresolved sexism, however, it becomes toxic. Very often, what plagues EBM and our intimate relationships is a sexism that's passed down through the umbilical chord.

Check out the following example. I can't even call it

an unpleasant exchange. By the time you turn thirty, you just accept that mothers reserve the right to occasionally say the most off-the-wall shit to their grown daughters—and get away with it. It's kind of "Come Out of Your Face for Free" card, I guess, for the time earned in the trenches. This is why I let my homegirl's moms get away with a remark that I would've excoriated any dude for.

"My daughter really has a wonderful life," said Mrs. Charles.* And she was right. Daphne Charles-Monroe* definitely does. Dee's like the Claire Huxtable of the crew. Not only is she fly as all hell, girlfriend managed to marry a handsome, gainfully employed black man who basically, as they say in the colloquium, *loves her dirty drawers.* In three short years they've acquired a beautiful house, dog, great kid, and car—*in that order.* And because theirs is the closest thing to a long-term, working relationship most of Dee's friends have ever seen, they've kinda become our role models.

So it was all good until Mrs. Charles said to me (Dee's very single and career-minded girlfriend), "I'm so glad that Daphne isn't like so many of these young women today. They're so selfish and absorbed in their

* Not her real name.

careers they don't even *know* how to treat a good man. No wonder they're all single." The air in Dee's huge, airy brownstone suddenly got too thick to breathe. Grateful for the stack of dirty dishes in the sink, I quickly found something else to do. Silently I rehearsed what I woulda said if I hadn't been so mad, hurt, and mindful of the fact that I'm supposed to respect my elders.

Dang, Mrs. C., I'm a little tired of our mothers bashing us for nothing more than growing and becoming the women you raised us to be. Remember? Highly independent, powerful, and truly unafraid to be our best? I mean correct me if I'm wrong but lessons on "How to Treat a Man" were not (thank God) part of the carefully planned education you all provided when we attended those "fine private schools and elite universities." In case you've forgotten, you and Mommy were all about: "You-all-better-not-be-concentrating-on-the-boys-or-majoring-in-MRS.-because-we're-not-sending-you-to-school-for-that-you-hear-me-you-girls-better-make-sure-you-get-good-educations-so-you-can-support-yourselves-and-not-be-waiting-around-for-some-man-to-do-it-for-you-I'm-serious."

This is what I remember: The endless mother/daughter theater parties and cultural events you all had us attend so we'd know we were "just as good as those white kids dammit, even better, because you girls are black and you had to work twice as hard to get to where you are—and don't you ever forget it."

You telling us over and over again to treat each other like sistas and NEVER let "some man come between you girls because the men will come and go but the friendships you girls have will last forever." The crew's still intact almost two decades later because we never did and they never have.

Pardon my French, Mrs. C., but I happen to think the way you guys raised us was the shit and I'm not going to let you or my single status make me feel bad about any of it. Loving my career as much as any ambitious dude loves his doesn't make me inordinately selfish. I just don't think it's too much to ask any brother who wants to be in the mix to respect and support my hustle.

Nothing personal, Mrs. C., but I kinda feel like before mothers start bashing their perpetually single career girls they might want to check themselves. After all, the brothers we date are the sons they raised. And I don't know if you've peeped this or not but highly independent, well-educated, intelligent, driven sistas are not always on the top of their list. Evidently we're a li'l more high maintenance than those oh-so-grateful chickenheads, who are basically grateful to sit up in the house, make babies, and go shopping.

It's like Gloria Steinem said. Our mothers did a great job raising their daughters to become the men they once wanted *to marry. But how about raising their sons to become the men their daughters need?*

"You cannot have an irresponsible man if he was not allowed to be an irresponsible boy," states Dr. Jawanza Kunjufu. "Some women raise their daughters and love their sons," he explains, referring to the markedly different ways some black women raise boys and girls. "They require little of their sons in the areas of household duties: taking care of siblings, going to church, or doing well in school, while their daughters are expected to excel in these areas. These mothers are creating totally dependent men who will expect all women to do for them. Yet these boys are future husbands and fathers." [4]

These are the men sistas are talking about when they claim black men can't deal with a strong-intelligent-independent-black-woman. It's even graver than expecting women to do all for them. Their mothers' failure to foster in them the same sense of responsibility and accountability that they demand of their daughters denies their sons the drive, determination, and overall stick-to-itiveness required to overcome obstacles. It also robs them of valuable self-esteem earned from meeting difficult challenges. Instead, these men learn to make excuses and wallow in a state of learned helplessness. In other words they *succumb* to being ENDAN-GERED.

And EBM are wholly incompatible with daughters raised to be strong women.

Further exacerbating the problem are those mothers whose perceptions of black manhood are not only informed by sexism but disappointment and low expectations. Women who maintain "all men are dogs" send dangerous messages to their sons. Whether it's their intention or not, passively accepting the mistreatment of women as a function of gender—as opposed to sexism and a lack of good home training—invariably condones the behavior. And the outcome can be emotionally devastating for all involved.

When Alexis* tells the tale of her boyfriend's infidelity she is visibly shaken. After dating Carl† for two years, they decided to live together. Alexis's parents paid for their apartment while they both attended grad school. "They saw I was really in love and that Carl was determined to make something of himself, so they let us live together.

"They've been there for him, for us, in every way. I

* Not her real name.
† Not his real name.

mean, we both worked, but if we needed groceries or money they sent enough for both of us. They treated him like a son."

During the course of their relationship, Carl got another woman pregnant. He didn't tell Alexis until after the baby was born. Although his mother was clearly upset and conflicted, in order to protect him, his family participated in a series of lies—of omission and otherwise—regarding everything from his relationship with the other woman to his general whereabouts.

"What hurt me more than anything," says Alexis, "was that as close as I supposedly was to his mother and his sisters, they didn't tell me. I don't understand how they could keep something like that from me. Three months maybe, but the whole nine?"

Although Carl claims he's in love and wants to continue the relationship, Alexis doubts she'll ever trust him _or_ his family. "Even if I could forgive him, I don't know if I could ever forgive _them_. How could I believe anything they tell me?"

Black women who turn a blind eye, laugh, or brag about their sons' many girlfriends (unacceptable antics, mind you, from their daughters), or assume collusive roles in their sons' doggish behavior have no right to complain about the lack of "good black men." What they need is to develop a greater sense of responsibility in their sons and to other black women.

Mothers play powerful roles in determining their sons' ability to respect women. Good black men don't just appear out of nowhere. They are nurtured, taught, and cultivated. There are many black women who raised their sons to be good, decent, responsible black men, who are in turn, good boyfriends, husbands, and fathers. However, when mothers allow their pain and lack of faith in black men to blind them to their own power the result is a vicious, unending cycle. Not only do they end up with ENDANGEREDBLACKMEN who lack the confidence and strength needed to withstand the daily assaults racism makes on black folks' spirits, their sons also bear painful resemblance to the very men who broke their hearts. And these sons grow into men who are bound to break the hearts of other black women's daughters.

Ultimately, healing relationships between black men and women depend on our ability to forgive. One of the most toxic by-products of black folks' history is an anger rooted in centuries of racism and human suffering. An anger black men and women, however unwittingly, are quick to turn on each other. It's time to acknowledge it, and then let it go. If not for our own sakes, then for the sakes of our children.

I'll leave you with the following bit of Marita Golden's sagacity: "The generations-old backlog of anger that African-American men and women hoard and revisit and unleash upon one another with a genius that is frightening becomes a script that our sons and daughters memorize, practicing its lethal intent and perfecting it in their own lives."

The only elixir she maintains, is forgiveness. "African-American women must forgive the real and imagined crimes of their sons' fathers. We must resist the urge to visit upon all the men in our lives the bitterness and pain planted by incompetent fathers or disappointing lovers. . . .

"And we must forgive black men for not protecting us against slavery, racism, white men, our confusion, or their doubts. And black men have to forgive black women for our own sometimes dubious choices, divided loyalties, and lack of belief in their possibilites."

Because "only when our sons and daughters know that forgiveness is real, existent, and that those who love them practice it, can they form bonds as men and women that really can save and change our community." [5]

Can I get an Amen?

lovenote

I think you better call Tyrone
And tell him come on and help you get your shit
— Erykah Badu, "Tyrone"

Happy Kwanzaa, Chica,
Ms. Badu Live, for your listening pleasure, from one SBW in
recovery to another. The first time I heard her perform "Tyrone"
was at a benefit for The Tea Party (Brooklyn's weekly black boho
fete) and knew it was a must-have for the nineties black girl

archives. Stick it next to your bootleg copies of Waiting to
Exhale *and* Soul Food.

*As soon as Erykah got through the first verse, I knew I was
about to have one of those "Damn, I wish my Dawg was here"
moments. Talk about the universality of the EBM (aka "Trifling
Nigga") experience. When girlfriend started droppin' the lyrics,
sistas lost their minds. So did the brothers, for that matter. It
was as if everybody had either been a Tyrone, that wack-ass
friend of Tyrone's, or a sista finally telling her EBM to "call
Tyrone and tell him to come on and help you get your shit."*

*As I watched Ms. Badu——in her eminent badness——do her
thing I caught myself wondering how some broke, cheap, all
dreams and no plan gwanna (as in "Gwanna do this," "Gwanna
do that") nigga managed to work his way into her fly-ass life.
That was until I remembered the times somebody might've
looked at my man (or yours) and wondered the same thing. One
thing's for sure, EBM manage to pull some of the baddest black
women around.*

*The funny thing, most of them aren't even on some suave
pimp shit. Most of the time, they're just regla brothers——cute,
nice, relatively well intentioned but altogether lacking in drive,
direction, and gumption. And you know I got mad sympathy for
the "Plight of the Black Man" but damn, racism (and sexism)
kicks our asses too and we still manage to get up and do what
we gotta. If EBM are pimping anything it's that damn
STRONGBLACKWOMAN conditioning of ours convincing us it's*

our righteous sista duty to help a black man reach his potential.

Girl, fuck potential. Nice, sweet, and well intentioned won't get a brother into Harvard if he's only got a C+ average. It won't get him into the NBA if he can't shoot for shit. It won't get him a six-figure salary at a top law firm if he can't pass the bar. But nice, sweet, and well intentioned will get a nigga some sympathetic pussy every time.

Not these drawers, darling. Not in the Nine Eight. Which brings me to my second gift. In the spirit of our mutual, ongoing quest for love, romance, happiness, and great sex I share with you '98's Relationship Resolutions. Smack me two times, if you catch me breaking them.

Forever Your Homey,
Joan

I will not be an SBW.

I mean it. If I'm buggin' 'cause my check is late, the mortgage is past due, and there are no groceries in the refrigerator, I'm gonna tell him the truth. If I need him to hold me at night 'cuz sometimes the past is too much and the future is too uncertain, I'm gonna tell him that too. Independence is one thing but fear is another. Fear will make ya front like Superwoman every time. Pretending to be totally self-sufficient is a helluva lot easier than handing your vulnerability over to a man who might drop the ball. But since carrying it on my own has damn sure worn me out, I'm gonna take a chance and TRUST somebody. What's the worst that can happen? At this stage in the game, me and Heartache are close enough to know it might hurt like a motha but it damn sure won't kill me. If some fool drops the ball, I'm just gonna pick my shit up, dust it off, and hand it to the man who can carry it.

I won't deal with ENDANGEREDBLACKMEN (or any black man whose lack of productivity I find myself explaining away with sociological injustice, childhood trauma, or basic hard-luck stories).

'Cuz I mean really, what's the point? A man who

ain't happy, can't make you happy. And like Mary said, happy's all I'm trying to be. I don't care what the songs say—my black woman's love (sweet as it is) can't save an EBM from himself. I still got love for my endangered brethren, no doubt—politically, culturally, and socially speaking. But people who work with alcoholics and crackheads don't give their unhealthy clients an open invitation into their bed, homes, and lives and I don't see why I should either. I finally realized that it's possible to love a brotha and encourage him to do better without handing out an all-access pass to my heart or the pooh. The next time some fine-ass EBM comes into my life and I'm even tempted to slide him some rhythm, my SBW in recovery ass is going to remember this: Kicking it with a man who has a ton of problems your love can't possibly solve is a great way NOT to deal with your own.

I'm gonna make the S-word in my relationships "Standards" instead of "Settle"—and I will not feel guilty about it.

A while back I was kicking it with this really sweet white dude and my girl asked me the "Is it true that white men treat you better than brothers" question. I thought she was tripping until I realized why she asked. Out of all the guys that were in the mix at the time—

147

and they were several—Sean* was the only white one and the only one I never complained about.

In truth, he was a darling. Fine. Charming as hell. Always called when he said he would. Exceptional home training. No games. Treated me like gold. Great job. Great family. Loads of ambition. Had the whole Ivy League/prep school thing going on. Just a real cool dude.

So it made sense that he was far less stress than oh, let's say that brother who was of the "ex-struggling promoter–aspiring producer–but presently working in a boutique" variety. Baby had tons of dreams, no plans, no scrilla but did have a kid, a babymother, and a really sick relationship with his mom. Oh, and did I mention no phone? His favorite pastime during our brief tenure together was telling me his problems from the pay phone in front of the bodega.

What didn't make sense is that I wouldn't have even thought about seeing a white guy who came in that package. Years of listening to my mom and her friends long-standing advice on interracial dating—"If You Girls Must Date These White Boys *Pulllease* Don't Come Home with Something Even the White Girls

---

* Not his real name.

Don't Want"—made certain things a given: If a white man wanted to get in the mix, he had to bring at least as much as I did to the table. My girl's observations were partially right. Sean did treat me better than several brothers I dated, but it wasn't because he was white. He simply had much more of himself to give.

When I tried to set the same criterion for brothers I'd feel guilty as hell. A "good black woman," I'd remind myself, is always aware of the impact of racism on brothers' self-esteem and shouldn't judge too harshly. In actuality, I'd fallen hard for alla that tired conditioning designed to make sistas feel like we're being classist, insensitive, and brainwashed by "The Man" just because we demand a brother have a legal hustle and three G's: goals, game plan, and good home training. Then I wondered why time that should've been spent getting back the same support I gave was instead spent trying to dispel some EBM's jealousy and insecurities by convincing him he really did deserve me?

I'm over it. The next time some dude tells me he doesn't deserve me, I'm gonna assume he knows what he's talking about and head toward the nearest exit. I've finally realized that it doesn't make me any less black, compassionate, or womanly to say a brother simply can't cut it. I happen to be a black woman who brings a lot to the table and I have a right to demand the same. I believe in myself, I want my man to believe in himself. I work hard, I want him to work hard. I love black folks, and life, and myself. And I want him to do the same. I don't ask for any more than I'm prepared and capable of giving. I set standards using myself as a measure of excellence—because anything else is just settling.

I will not fall in love with a man's potential.

When it comes to romance, sistas need to eliminate the words "if only" from our vocabulary. What Dude will be in five years "if only" he got therapy, healed his relationship with his mother, stopped tricking bitches, eased up on his hustle, focused, or got over his commitment anxiety is really none of our business. Potential is a relationship between an individual and God. When it comes to life's lessons, people learn the lesson when they're damn good and ready to receive it—and that's usually not a second before the good Lord sees fit. All the loving, pushing, willing, cajoling, nagging, or threatening in the world won't get two-year-olds to act like they're twelve. And it doesn't work on grown men either.

When it comes to me and love, unrealized potential

has been rendered wholly irrelevant. Because even if a man becomes all the wonderful things you believe he can be, there's absolutely no guarantee that he'll become them *with you*. In all likelihood, it's the sista whose standards won't allow her to settle for anything less that's going to end up with that finished product. So instead of focusing on what I think a man *could* become, I'm going to ask the only relevant question: Is this man, with all his faults, capable of making me happy *right now?*

I will not spend time with men I don't respect.

I'm not just talking about on an intimate level, I mean this across the board. I've got a girlfriend who spends a lot of time hanging out with married men and their mistresses. Then she wonders why she doesn't trust men as far as she can throw them. I've found that the best way to keep from being an angry, distrustful black woman is to simply keep the best possible specimens of the gender around me. For that reason all the lovers, friends, exes, brothers, and cousins that occupy prime space in my life all meet the same prerequisite: The way these men live their lives—the care they bestow on their children, the honor they show their parents, the faithful way they love their women, the superior way they execute their hustle—makes me repeatedly say, "Damn, that's how I want to be." And the particular way we love each other makes us better people.

I will not spend all my time hanging out with women that don't respect men.

Constantly finding myself participating in those perennial men-bashing sessions means I'm obviously doing something wrong: like commiserating with sistas who are just as clueless as I am about how to have a healthy relationship. From now on, I'm checking for the sista whose marriage is so tight, relationship so bangin', or single status so fulfilling that she has very little to say on the topic. I wanna find out what she's doing right and follow her example.

I'm going to make God the main man in my life.

When me and God's relationship is right, everything else just kinda falls into place. If work feels like it's demanding too much, I kick it with God and he reminds me of my purpose. If life's obstacles seem too much for me to handle, God wraps his arms around me and reminds me of what we've accomplished together in the past. If loneliness is tempting me to lay my heart down in a place it can't helped but get stepped on, God reminds me that heartache is what tends to set in when a woman calls on a man to do the job that was intended only for Him.

Fulfilling a hunger for a love unconditional, one that never abandons or disappoints, one that replaces the imperfect love of a flawed parent or never fails to come through in our time of need is a very heavy task. And a damn near impossible assignment for creatures made of mere flesh and blood. That kind of loving is best provided by a divine and perfect Spirit. By giving God his proper place, I free my relationships from unreasonable expectations. And I free myself from fear—because I know that somebody out there has got my back. Regardless.

babymother

I tried not to stare at her, this woman the color of Cadbury chocolates. She was alternately laughing and mumbling to herself while rocking back and forth. Of course, not staring was a courtesy she'd failed to extend. Just seconds before, her large brown eyes traced my profile intrusively, outlined its unruly kinky curls, examined the curve of my neck, lingered for a moment at my breasts and hands with a slightly crazed intensity.

"Watcha doing?" she asked loudly with a hint of cynicism. "Typing?"

My response, an acerbic *I'm writing* followed by a silent *Stupid* prompted her to read loudly from my computer screen as if it were the most natural thing in the world. With the malicious innocence typical of the insane, Miss Chocolate shouts my pathetic attempts at a new chapter for everyone in the writer-infested coffeehouse to hear. *Look,* I warn silently, *I don't give a fuck if you're crazy or not, you're 'bout two seconds away from an ass-whooping.* Meeting my glare with callous laughter, she shifted her gaze to the window.

Only then did I truly see her. The tufts of jet-black hair growing between once meticulously parted cornrows like triumphant weeds laying claim to a garden. Her baby-doll dress—an orange, worn, and faded thing —covered with the kind of polka dots favored by toddlers and circus clowns. The remnants of baby powder floating against the dark canvas of her arms and shoulders, like cirrus clouds across an expansive sky.

I realize I can't figure out anything about her: how old she is, if she was once pretty. If she likes boys or girls. If she's ever had sex. If the older, Jheri-curled black woman sitting next to her is a home attendant or her mother. The older woman offers no clues. Instead, she passes time circling passages from the Bible, ignoring Miss Chocolate with the dispassion of those God grants the serenity to accept what cannot be changed. Unlike me, she doesn't flinch when Miss Chocolate suddenly starts praying with Pentecostal fervor for Jesus to give her a son. *Please, Jesus, please, Jesus, everything would be okay if I could just have a baby. Sweet baby Jesus, please give me a son.*

Her caretaker's apathy underscored the inherent irony in insanity. Repeated often enough, even the most aberrant acts bear a striking resemblance to normalcy.

"Do you think Jesus heard me?" Miss Chocolate asks as they finally prepare to leave. "Yes," answers the older woman wearily, closing her Bible. "Good," says Miss Chocolate. "Then it'll get done."

As the issues of black women, desire, and babies become unwitting constants in my life, memories of Miss Chocolate invade my thoughts often. Despite her craziness, I marvel at the bold clarity of her desire to be a mother. For me it was never this way.

Maternal instinct has been a dark shadow slowly illuminated by unexpected moments—recently flickering into my consciousness like the soft warm lights of tiny candles. Touching the protruding bellies of my two best friends during their simultaneous pregnancies. Marveling over the details of their daughters' dramatic entries into this world—Damali's marked by willful, deliberate stubbornness and Noni's with ridiculous ease and flair—telltale imprints of the women their mothers already are and the little girls they are quickly becoming. The gentleness of the unsolicited kiss one bestows on my cut finger. The absolute sense of peace I feel when the other falls asleep in my arms. The new friend's knowing smile as I confess all this. The achingly tender way his mammoth brown arms cradles them as he inhales, smiles, and imagines their smell—the three or five kids he plans to have some day. The undeniable melt of age-old glaciers that once surrounded my heart.

Still, the arrival of my previously comatose instincts is marked with anxiety. The very idea of surrendering an identity defined solely by me (and to a large degree by my profession) for one so completely defined by someone else—my child and my husband—terrifies me. I feel like the career bitch from hell every time I hear my girlfriends say they would gladly abandon careers to be full-time mothers and housewives. But I watched my mother's life literally blossom after she put herself through college and started to support herself in the career of her choice. Through her example, I learned that a career wasn't only about financial survival but about freedom, self-esteem, and identity. Unlike so many of my childhood friends, I grew up unafraid to dream. My mother was proof positive that with hard work and sacrifice anything was attainable.

I want the same for my daughter. I want her to know that her legacy is a willingness to fight, to play hard and win, and find love in everything she does. And I believe that gift will be invaluable.

Despite my apparent convictions, however, I'm susceptible to the sexist but popular myth that defines a good mother as selfless and giving—easily subsuming her own needs for the well-being of her children. I know I am no such creature. Nurturing, giving, loving, kind, understanding, and patient—yes. Ambitious, driven, and competitive—definitely. In a father this is considered a perfect combination, but as a woman I'm cautioned against the impossibility of "having it all."

Denying I want it all, however, is futile. I've never been good at settling for anything less.

I'm also terrified of going it alone in a world where single motherhood for black women is quickly becoming a norm. I'm haunted by the multitude of stats that cruelly remind me that my daughter has only a slim chance of growing up with two married parents attending her Sweet Sixteen. I'm sick of those who deny me this fear—all those who give my life a perfunctory glance, perceive a certain degree of financial stability and advise me "to just go on and do it, girl, 'cuz you don't need no man." Dumb tired of explaining that my desire to have children doesn't stem from sheer biological necessity. I *want* to be part of a healthy, loving, two-parent black family—for reasons that are as political as they are personal.

"What are you waiting for, girl?" The question falls from the sista's mouth so effortlessly, I instinctively glance at the ring finger of my left hand. No, I assure myself. It is still empty. No wedding band has mysteriously appeared. To her knowledge and mine, I am still unmarried. Nevertheless, she repeats herself, stating her case more strongly. "You got the job, the house—when are you going to have a baby?" My answer, that I am waiting to be married, launches her into a lengthy diatribe that starts with reasons I don't need no man and ends with the historical strength of black women.

Her attitude is one of the reasons I've come to dread these things. I'm all for high-level sista-girl camaraderie but the incumbent protocol of the "babymother" shower gets to me. There is so much one is required not to admit. Amidst the Afrocen*chic* party favors and sympathetically generous gifts I think of Miss Chocolate's naive belief that a tiny, helpless, needy baby can bring order to an existence fraught with chaos. And I wonder how many single, sane, and pregnant black women once thought the same. Why (whether we admit this or not), in spite of feminism, fine educations, professional accomplishments, and an abundance of evidence to the contrary, do so many sistas still believe that babies and mothers are package deals, that they will be the magical love glue that permanently binds us to a man who never intended to stay.

There used to be plausible explanations. This was back when I was a teenager and the 'hood was full of girls who knew too much about poverty, violence, and loss, and too little about the possibilities of life outside the ghetto. Unconditional love was a little-known delicacy, and pregnancy allowed them to at least taste the potential. But I'm no longer a shorty in the 'hood. My peers are formidable black women—bright, ambitious, employed, degreed, and in most cases, very easy on the eyes.

Despite these facts, the number of baby showers I've attended in the last two years has outnumbered bridal showers three to one. Contrary to popular class biases, this is hardly a "ghetto" phenomenon. (Twenty-two percent of black women making upwards of $75,000 a year become single parents—ten times the number of white ones.[1]) In stark contradiction to the feminist hype —the accomplished super-sista who is not pressed about being married, has reached a certain age, has made substantial loot, and got pregnant intentionally— the event is often unplanned, in the midst of unstable or nonexistent relationships and accompanied by mad drama.

But we will talk about none of this. Instead, we'll spend the afternoon recounting survival tales of strong black women who've successfully undertaken the monumental task of parenting alone. Conspicuously absent from these conversations are testimonies of the heartache experienced when one's partner declines to share in the ups and downs of pregnancy and parenting. No stories will be told about the black women who've succumbed to the very real pressures of single parenting —among them constant emotional and financial strain, day-to-day uncertainty about the future, and the relinquishing of lifelong dreams. You know, the sistas we tend to *tsk, tsk* when they abandon their children at the local mall.

Instead we'll reassure the mother to be that she can "do it" becuz the absence of a committed black father (let alone husband) is as common as a fish in the sea.

Repeated often enough, Miss Chocolate reminds me, *even the most aberrant acts can seem strikingly, dangerously normal.*

Succumbing to the dynamics of peer pressure and protocol, I refrain from telling the sista a few things. Among them that strong, black women of the past did not parent solo because they wanted to—the conditions that ruled their lives do not, thank God, rule mine. I am not a slave, and there is no caseworker breaking up my family, abortion is no longer illegal, and I have more options for birth control than I even know what to do with. That as a daughter still healing from the wounds inflicted by my own father's absenteeism—injuries which once made me doubt my suitability for lifetime commitment at all—I'll be damned if I'd willingly subject my daughter to the same. Besides, I've seen the bravado of that "My baby, my body, I don't need *him*" attitude dissipate quickly with the realities of "babymotherhood." Seen it more times than I care to remember.

Suffice it to say that raising a family is perhaps the only area of my life where I'm not afraid to admit I *need* a man. Still, despite the preponderance of sistas allegedly waiting to exhale, I often feel like I'm in the minority.

The black family—historically one of our most critical support systems—is perilously close to becoming an endangered species. As of 1994, 70 percent of black children were born to unmarried women (versus 25 percent of white children) and only 33 percent of black children lived with both parents (versus 76 percent of white ones).[2]

All praises given to black single mothers who've consistently managed to do the best with what little they have. But denying that single parenting takes a toll on our community is an exercise in futility. The correlation between single-parent homes, teenage pregnancy, crime, and poverty have been demonstrated ad nauseam.

"Children of single mothers are significantly more likely to live in poverty than children living with both parents," states a special edition of *Newsweek* magazine darkly entitled "A World Without Fathers: The Struggle to Save the Black Family." According to 1990 census figures, the article states, "65% of black single mothers were poor, compared with only 18% of children of black married couples." And "educationally, children of one-parent families are at greater risk across the board for learning problems, for being left back, for dropping out. . . . By every measure—economic, social, educational," the article concludes, the statistics strongly indicate that "two parents living together are better than one." [3]

Perhaps one of the most revolutionary acts the hip-hop generation can accomplish is to establish healthy, loving, functional families. On certain levels we are aware of this. We watched a million marching men get the message in Washington. Our griots' rhymes—Tupac's "Keep Your Head Up," Naughty by Nature's "Ghetto Bastard," and the intro of *Ready to Die* by the Notorious B.I.G. to name a few—repeatedly demonstrate painful awareness of the impact fractured family structures have on our lives. The epidemic levels of single parenting, however, indicate a reluctance to move past lip service to action. Overall, our response has been frightfully anemic—fluctuating between defeatist denial and apathetic acceptance.

For far too many of us, the absence of a committed black father is "just the way things are."

We are not entirely to blame. Coming of age in the eighties and nineties, the hip-hop generation is caught in the quagmire of conflicting social, moral, and political values that typify American society at the close of this millennium. Our elders left us a lot of mixed messages. Older heads spent the sixties and seventies enjoying "Free Love," but we reaped the repercussions of the Sexual Revolution—among them the devastating advent of AIDS, a one-out-of-two divorce rate, and waning value for the cornerstones of a stable society: monogamy, marriage, and the nuclear family.

The few road maps bequeathed to us are often too confusing to be useful. In the name of free speech, freedom of expression, and ultimately, the Almighty Dollar, sexually explicit images bombard us daily. Yet we're instructed to cope with AIDS's senseless destruction by practicing the sexual conservatism of our grandparents. Abstinence (if you can stand it), safe sex (at the very least), and monogamy (whenever you can). Most of us, however, haven't got a clue as to how to achieve the latter. We can count the number of healthy marriages or lasting relationships we've seen on one hand.

Is it any wonder Naughty by Nature's "O.P.P." (Other People's Property) became the sexual anthem for the nineties? With our fear of intimacy and our disbelief in monogamy pushing it steadily along, the record transcended vinyl and became culture.

The situation for young brothers and sistas is even more hectic. Our skepticism when it comes to "forevers" and " 'til death do we part" is not at all unfounded. "The institution of marriage [for blacks]," cites *Newsweek,* "has been devastated in the last generation. . . . As of 1992, only 38% of black women were married——a significant decline from the '60s, when more than 60% of young black women between the ages of 20–24 were married."[4] For black women who live with these odds daily, the growing tendency to view brothers as optional parts of the parenting equation is less about a lack of desire than about refusing to be stuck with a proverbial case of sour grapes. Why waste time wishing on what you know you'll never have?

According to hip-hop tour de force Bill Stephney, one of the visionary powers behind the seminal rap group Public Enemy, president of Step-Sun Records, and the activist behind the formation of F.O.L.A. (Families Organized for Liberty and Action), society's shifting attitudes about not only marriage but about sex, birth control, abortion, welfare, and ultimately child support and paternity laws add tremendously to the confusion many single black men experience when facing fatherhood.

"It's hard for a man today to figure out what his role is supposed to be," explains Stephney, who was a single father until getting married a few years ago. "There was a time in African-American history when marriage was an important value in the *community*. As a man, you felt you had a *moral* responsibility to a child born out of wedlock—partially because there was enough societal pressure on a man who got a woman pregnant to marry her. That was 'being responsible.'

"Culturally we've moved away from that. There's a lot of confusion regarding what being responsible actually means. Does 'being responsible' to a pregnant woman mean rubbing her stomach and bringing her ice cream when she has cravings, or does it mean marrying her? Or does it mean paying her $10,000 a year in child support?

"Even when a man says he wants to be as morally, ethically, spiritually, and loving as he can, there seems to be so much of a preponderance on finance that it pretty much bursts your bubble right there."

Sistas feeling that "black men are irrelevant when it comes to raising our children," cautions Stephney, "only serves to widen the chasm between us.

"Take a brother who's struggling. Of course he goes berserk when he hears homegirl's pregnant. He feels marginalized because everything around him is saying he has no role in that creation we consider so precious other than being informed that the baby's coming and how much money he's expected to pay."

Truth be told, society on a whole is suffering the effects of both feminism's and the government's failure to tackle the lack of men's choices when it comes to reproductive and parental rights. Any pro-choice feminist worth her salt (self included) could not conceive of endorsing legislation that would allow a man's desire to be a father take precedence over the mother's unwillingness to carry the child to term. We recognize her exclusive right to control her body and consequently her destiny. In fact, we're ballistic about it.

When it comes to admitting, however, that the struggle for female independence and reproductive choice also grants women the power *to control the lives and destinies of unwilling fathers via their bodies,* feminism conveniently tosses the goal of a gender-equal society out the window. It plunges instead head-first into a cesspool of hypocrisy—embracing the very same sexist stereotypes it should be fighting against.

• • •

Take the case of Layla* and Glenn.† Layla, a twenty-nine-year-old trial attorney, met Glenn, a thirty-year-old graphic artist, through a mutual friend. They'd seen each other at a few parties following their initial meeting and immediately developed the hotties. They slept together once, on their first date, and things were left open-ended.

A few weeks later, Layla discovered she was pregnant. Engaged to someone else, Glenn begged Layla not to have the baby. Furthermore, he warned her in no uncertain terms he'd have nothing to do with her or the child. But at twenty-nine, with a decent job and guaranteed support from friends and family, Layla felt abortion and adoption were not options she could entertain in good conscience—even if it meant no emotional or financial support from the child's father.

So following the script written for her by decades of feminist struggle, Layla ignored Glenn's pleas, exercised her right to choice, and demanded nothing from him—except child support—once the child was born. Both Glenn and his fiancée adamantly refused. Already stretched financially, they were expecting their first

* Not her real name.
† Not his real name.

child in six months, and felt they simply could not afford it.

Furthermore, Glenn felt Layla's decision to bring a child into the world with a man she barely knew was not only ludicrous but selfish. "It was all about *her* body, *her* choice, and what was best for her life. She didn't give a damn that she was turning my life upside down. Layla's last words to me were that she and the baby didn't need me. And now I'm expected to pay child support?"

Okay. So we all agree Glenn is less than a mensch, but you gotta admit his contentions pose a sticky challenge to those of us who are supposedly down for equality. How can a feminism that vehemently supports women's right to reproductive choice support indiscriminate child-support laws which force men to be financially responsible for children they may not have wanted?

A woman's right to reproductive choice is about more than controlling her body—it constitutionally imbues her with the right *not to parent*. It encourages her to honestly evaluate her feelings about parenting and her abilities to do so. If for any reason she doesn't feel up to the task, she has the legal right to terminate her pregnancy or give her child up for adoption.

Men's anxieties and doubts about parenting are dismissed, however, as illegitimate and irresponsible behavior. An expectant father expressing any reluctance about becoming a parent is pretty much branded a dog. Furthermore, he's legally denied all of the options granted to an expectant mother. He can't force a woman to have an abortion, he can't abdicate his parental rights (via adoption) without the mother's consent, and he must pay child support.

The inconsistencies are glaring. If feminists honestly believe that forcing unwilling mothers into parenthood isn't in the best interests of mothers or children, why aren't fathers given the same consideration? Both genders are equally necessary for reproduction and they should be entitled to similar rights. One of the greatest mistakes of the Feminist Movement is its misrepresentation of reproductive rights. Reproductive rights, including the right not to parent is not a *woman's* right. It's a *human* one.

Denying that men should have the same option not to parent is hypocritical and it threatens the goal of gender equality.

"It's quite literally the idea of the 'baby's mama' and whatever support daddy can lend," maintains Stephney. "As a society we've moved from the notion of wives and children as property as experienced during common law, to the notion of children as mother's property. Instead of making mothers second-class citizens, we make fathers second-class citizens by arguing that they're optional.

"Even the court systems seemed to have determined that the obligatory roles fathers have is financial (something we would never say about mothers), which is really wrong. Do you mean all the things I could be for my child's entire lifetime can be made irrelevant based on how much money I'm making?

"As a black man it insults me from a human standpoint and a historical one. Certainly our sharecropping grandfathers' value to their families was not based on money."

Whether you agree with Stephney's assessment or not, it's clear that feminism's unwillingness to confront the highly complex issues that accompany the movement's most significant advances—specifically birth control, legalized abortion, and child support and paternity laws—has left its daughters to sort out the mess.

Ultimately, the issue of male reproductive rights is one that forces women to face some of the yuckier by-products of our quest for power. If the goal is a balanced distribution of power between men and women, then both genders have to relinquish their vise-grip on their respective domains. For men that means workplace and the wallet. For women, however, it means being less territorial when it comes to the domain of the family. Refusing to see fathers' participation as optional puts us one step closer to eradicating those nasty patriarchal stereotypes of family (men as providers and women as child rearers and nurturers)—and all their sexist implications. Elevating the role fathers play so that it's as intrinsically valuable as the role of mothers would be infinitely more productive than sitting around, trying to convince each other that "we don't need no man."

Next on the agenda should be a re-evaluation of mandatory child-support and paternity laws. Both feminism and government need to understand that child-support checks can't take the place of a father's active participation in his child's life.

One option that seems to be gaining increased support is enforced joint custody. Sonny Burmeister, president of the Children's Rights Council of Georgia, and Mary Frances Berry, author of *The Politics of Parenthood*, are both advocates of enforced joint physical custody between unmarried parents. "A court decree," states

Berry, "should require not just child-support payments, but burden sharing or shifting to take care of the children in order to impress upon both parties the seriousness of their obligation. Neither fathers nor mothers should be able to walk away without some pressure being brought to bear." Ideally, she suggests, parents should have "shared custody." In cases where this is not possible, the non-custodial parent "should also be required to help the other with chores that drain custodial parents of time and energy, such as baby-sitting, transportation to doctor's appointments and other child-care services or to school." [5]

Burmeister, however, believes that under a system of joint custody, no one should pay child support: "Why would you need a transfer of money," he asks, "if you each have the child for fifteen days?" [6] And Stephney agrees. "It shouldn't even be a question of finance. There should be immediate joint custody. And the state should have no input unless there is total disagreement between two parties."

Before sistas dismiss these ideas as the mere foolishness of men too cheap to do right by their children, we might want to face the bleak statistical realities of "mandatory" child support. Unless your baby's father is paid as hell, your chances of collecting any money worth talking about are very slim. "The Child Support Enforcement program is a very expensive way to collect money and is notoriously ineffective when dealing with unmarried fathers," states Ellis Cose in his book *A Man's World: How Real Is Male Privilege—and How High Is Its Price?* "A Congressional Research Service calculated that in 1991 states netted $384 million from the program, while the federal government lost $588 million. The program, in short, cost $204 million more to run than it managed to bring in." [7]

And "while three-fourths of divorced women are granted child-support payments, only one-fourth of never-married mothers are awarded payments, and only three-fourths of those see any portion of the money." The average amount collected annually, according to this study, is barely Pamper money. It's in "the neighborhood of $2,000." [8]

Add to this fiasco that babymothers who apply for welfare automatically "assign their support rights to the state which only gives them up to fifty dollars a month of anything collected from the fathers of their children." [9]

"It doesn't take a Wharton grad," says Tom Henry of the Philadelphia Children's Network, "to figure out that a woman gets significantly more money if the father provides it directly (albeit covertly) to the mother than to the state."

Henry's colleague Ralph Smith feels that "the system has its priorities scrambled." The emphasis on money instead of participation may actually be driving these fathers away. "If society endeavored to get them attached to their kids as opposed to trying to confiscate their money, many of these young fathers would do the same things that the rest of us do," says Smith. "They [would] begin to find ways to provide the support their children need. And not all of the support their children need is financial support."

Despite the obvious merits to enforced joint custody, it's still problematic. It would be difficult to enforce— especially between parents whose relationships are funky or non-existent. It also skirts the very compli- cated issue of *male* reproductive rights. A woman who proceeds with a pregnancy against her partner's wishes has every right to do so. But should she have the right to force another human being into something as life altering as parenting? If we don't allow a father's desire for parenthood to impinge on an unwilling mother's desire for an abortion, how then, both legally and mor- ally, can we ignore an unwilling father's objections to parenthood?

According to law professor Melanie G. McCulley, we can't. McCulley has advocated legislation that would allow men faced with an unwanted pregnancy the legal right to abdicate their parental rights up until the first six months after the child's birth. She cites the unwillingness of courts to recognize and protect the "procreative choice" of the reputed father of a child born out of wedlock and has drafted a model statute that would protect the rights of the putative father. The statute would address situations in which a woman has not chosen adoption or abortion and wants to keep the child. Ordinarily, the putative father would have no say in whether to assume financial responsibilities to the child. The statute represents an attempt to balance the freedom of the woman to choose without interference from the would-be father, and the putative father's freedom not to become a parent.

Furthermore, under the statute, once the babydaddy has abdicated his parental rights—which include, by the way, the right to "custody," "companionship," "disciplinary action," managing the kid's money, or teaching her right and wrong—he should also be free of all financial responsibility—pretty much for the very same reasons we don't hold birth mothers financially responsible after their children have been adopted. If, however, the babydaddy failed to abdicate his rights, then child support would be mandatory.

Needless to say, many of the sistas I spoke with found McCulley's ideas anywhere from dangerous to bananas. Even the most pro-choice women shared their objections: *But suppose the woman can't have an abortion for moral, religious, or health reasons,* they countered. Or *suppose he was having unprotected sex? He made the decision that he was willing to have a baby the second he slid up inside her without a condom on.* More than a few suggested that *men need time to "come around"* to an initially unwanted pregnancy. Supposedly, allowing them to *just sign away their responsibilities* lets them off the hook too early and too easily.

All of these would be valid points in a society where abortion and adoption are *not* legal options. But in our society *they are.* None of the women in the above scenarios were denied choice. Religious reasons, moral and health reasons don't eliminate choice. While they are certainly valid reasons not to undergo an abortion, they don't rule out the possibilities of adoption.

The reactions are understandable. In a society still wrestling with the morality of abortion rights, the idea of men being able to abdicate their parental rights is a difficult one to swallow. Even more disconcerting is the legitimate fear that empowering men with reproductive choice and parental rights will place an unfair financial burden on innocent children. Ultimately, women will have to ask themselves if a truly gender-equal society is what we really want. In the meantime, any sista seriously considering proceeding with a pregnancy against the father-to-be's wishes should evaluate her ability to do so emotionally, spiritually, *and financially.* Because whether the laws reflect this or not, the logical and, yes, feminist extension of *my body, my baby, my choice* is *my sole financial responsibility.*

Fortunately, there are far less painful alternatives. As the old saying goes, an ounce of prevention is worth a pound of cure. For starters, we can confront how we feel about abortion, adoption, and unplanned pregnancy before sex.

Recognizing my own inability to consider abortion or adoption, for example, forced me to change up my program when it came to sex and my relationships. Understanding that any man I slept with could potentially be the father of my child (after all, the only foolproof form of birth control is abstinence) made me much more selective. *Fine* and *nice* and *just a li'l sump'n sump'n* are no longer enough to qualify. Now I have to ask myself if the brother is emotionally, spiritually, financially *capable* of being a good father. And since this is an evaluation that takes more than a few weeks . . . suffice it to say it takes me a good, long while before I'm ready to hit the sheets these days—if I hit them at all.

Since the decision to have a child ultimately rests with women, I think it's only fair for me to let my partner know my feelings beforehand. I need to know if he's down to parent at all, let alone parent *with* me. If he's not, and we can't see eye to eye, then I'm willing to explore other options. Sex, after all, isn't the only road to intimacy.

I'm not saying this is an easy topic to broach. After all, getting knocked up is hardly a pre-seduction topic —but sistas owe it to themselves, their partners, and their unborn children to have this discussion long before they hit the sheets. The AIDS epidemic taught our generation to be proactive when it came to sex. Demanding that our lovers use condoms and engaging in candid discussions about sexual history were habits women had to form if we intended to save our lives. If we can be that thorough when faced with the solemnity of death, we can do it with something as precious as new black lives.

We have to. Our survival depends on it.

chickenhead envy

Alright, Ms. Chicken,

We both know you and I don't particularly like each other, but it's time for a meeting of the minds. I confess, I'm a longtime Chickenhater—one of the smart, successful, hard-working, educated, super-independent black girls who spends a lot of time dissing you and your chickenhead sistren. In particular, we abhor your abject materialism, your predilection for Ricki Lake skankwear, and the nauseating way you stroke the male ego. For the record, none of us are buying that "airhead" shit. Any fool that's seen you in dick pursuit knows you can be calculating, cunning, and savvy as hell. Trust me, baby girl, if I ever lost my press pass and needed to get backstage, you are the first one I'd enlist. We just can't understand why, with all those skills, your sole ambition in life seems to be the wife (or babymother) of somebody who makes enough chedda to satisfy your shopping jones.

Admittedly we criticize you from extremely lofty perches. Convinced in our feminist, womanist, STRONGBLACKWOMAN principles we remind ourselves that we CHOSE to get educations, dedicate ourselves to our careers, cultivate not only our intellect but our spirits. We are the "good black women." We are the women our mothers and grandmothers dreamed they could be—professional, driven, fiercely independent, and free from men's financial control. We make men RESPECT our intellect, dreams, and ambitions. And for the most part, they do. So what does it matter if you got a man, a house, a car, and a big phat monthly allowance, and we seem to be perpetually single?

The difficult, shitty truth is that it matters much more than we'd like to admit. See, when we bought into the whole independent, successful, black girl thing, none of us ever dreamed we might end up alone. Granted the whole eighties—nineties "power couple" hype was probably some white folks' shit we shouldn't have bought into. But part of what got us through the inescapable hard times that came with our determination to succeed was the honest belief that successful

BMWs (Black Men Working) would be part of the payoff.
Instead, Ms. Chicken, it seems a good number of them are
ending up in your bed——and complaining to us about you.

Hell yeah, we're pissed about it.

I know this is a little foul. After all, it's not your fault these
otherwise smart brothers can't seem to see past the
big-ass-big-titties-jiggy-good-looks and deal with the obvious:
Without the magnetic chick pull of a well-laced wallet, most of
you would not give these boys the time of day. But to be honest
with you, sistas like me ain't trying to hear a brother grieving
over the expensive vacations, designer clothes, or the ten tennis
bracelets he bought you before you left him for a bigger Willy.
We don't wanna hear about the exorbitant amount of money
courts are forcing him to pay you for the baby he never wanted
to have. Not when we're single, paying our own rent, busting
our asses at work, and living for sample sales.

I confess, we may be dealing with an inflated sense of
entitlement here. Despite our knowledge that black Prince
Charmings are rare indeed, we do feel that if anybody's going to
end up with one, it should be one of us. As hard as we work, we
deserve them. It's not like we're exactly ideologically opposed to
nice homes, jewelry, shopping sprees, and some semblance of
financial security. We might not be waiting around for some
man to relieve us from a lifetime of work, but I don't know
many of us who wouldn't welcome the option. For real.

Quiet as it's kept, Ms. Chicken, essentially you, me, your

girls, my girls—we all want the same thing—someone to love us, shower us with attention, nurture and provide for us and our kids. The hatred we have for your chickenhead asses is in part the mask of bravado we wear to camouflage our fears. In our loneliest and most vulnerable moments, we look at you and wonder if chickenheads aren't the ones who have figured it all out. Is being alone the price we will ultimately pay for doing it the "right way"?

Or is it the penalty we'll pay for seeing a bit of ourselves in you—and fronting like we didn't. . . .

Chickenhead Envy is not a pretty thing. My first attack left me laid out—in fetal position—sobbing like Toni Braxton in the "Unbreak My Heart" video. One of my best friends in the world stood close by in helpless, empathetic silence. She was visibly shaken by her futile attempts to console me—and wholly afraid of leaving me alone. The sudden banging on my front door provided a temporary distraction.

"Joan!! JOAN!!" the voice hollered. "Are you okay? Let me in!!"

Who the . . ? Slowly it registered through my delirium. *Damn.* It was Dude. The one I'd been sleeping with (but not the one I liked). The one I'd warned repeatedly that there was no reason on God's green earth ever good enough to make surprise appearances at my door. The one (if I'd been a better person at the time) I woulda cut off months before, when I first realized the imbalance in our levels of affection. But among his many nocturnal delights was an insatiable seafood jones—we're talking won't stop eating 'til *you* get enough—and unfortunately, it thwarted any attempts at altruism.

Like an angel of mercy my girl's svelte but muscular

5′11″ frame staunchly barricaded the apartment door. "I must've called when whatever it is was all going down," he tried to explain. "I know she doesn't like people to just drop by, but she sounded so fucked-up."

"Yes, something's happened but you can't see her right now," my homey says kindly but with unchallenge-able resolve. She knew his worries were sweet but useless. He's not the one I like (the one I wasn't sleep-ing with). He's not calling to say, "It was all a lie. I do not have a girl at home that's six months pregnant—a fact I've neglected to mention for at least the last five." He's not the one who hurt me.

"Yes, she'll be alright," she assures him, while gently guiding him outside. "But she's in no condition to talk right now. *To anybody.*"

She returns to the couch and rubs my back sooth-ingly. Slowly, the tenderness of her caress converts my wailing to a soft, steady whimper. It doesn't, however, mask her confusion. And I am of no assistance. For the life of me, I can't tell her why her girl, someone whose response to severe emotional hurt is usually of the "Find him. Go to his home, office, gym, whatever, and scream, holler, and throw things, but whatever you do —fight" variety is lying catatonic on the sofa, teetering dangerously close to the abyss.

Mercifully, the only soul capable of doing me any earthly good calls unexpectedly. Carefully, gently she pulls me back from the precipice.

Bethann, I sniffle. *I just feel so stupid.*

"Stop it now. 'Cuz feelings are what they are, and we ain't gonna judge feelings."

I can't believe I let myself be played like that.

"It doesn't mean none of that, baby. This doesn't mean he doesn't care. It just means he didn't know how to tell you."

He's a fucking dick.

"Right now. Yes. And maybe tomorrow. But after a while you're going to have to let yourself remember the magic of him. Or this will eat you up inside."

I hurt, BA.

"Of course you do, baby. And believe it or not he does too. Nobody 'cept the devil could want to know he's tearing you up this bad inside."

The wisdom in this starts me blubbering again, and this time for a really, really long time. BA just listens. She doesn't even mention what I already know. That at some point we're going to have to talk about *my* responsibility in all this. 'Cuz even though this fool screwed up royally, I was grown enough to know that all the "Gwanna leaves" in the world don't alter this fact: Until the day he really broke clean he was always somebody else's. She does remind me that given the circumstances there was no other way for it to end—whether he'd been honest with me or not. The Joan she knows would never want a man who could turn his back on his pregnant babymother to go start something else. Of course this makes me feel better and then, simultaneously worse, because one of the things I love most about this man is his loyalty and sense of honor.

But mostly BethAnn waits for the epiphany, for me to realize that what I'm suffering from is not a broken heart, but a full-blown case of Chickenhead Envy. And the only cure is for me to confront the sordid, green-eyed source of my pain.

It was something I could only admit to a woman who loves me like a daughter. I really hadn't spent the last four hours crying because Dude betrayed our friendship and straight-up lied to me. I wasn't even mad that he was sleeping with his woman. I was mad and hurt that she was his woman at all.

Igniting my fury were the memories of endless conversations about his frustrations with a woman who seemed to have no greater life aspirations than being wifey. He paid her bills. Showered her with shopping sprees at Barneys. Handed over the keys to the Land

Cruiser. He just wanted—correction—needed her to want something out of life besides him.

I remembered the pride and interest he took in my work, the way he marveled at my independence and self-sufficiency and the encouragement he provided every time I tentatively shared a new goal. But I also remembered the exasperation in his voice as he confided, "Yo, I tell her all the time, you want to go to school? I'll pay for it. You wanna start a business? I'll finance it, but all this free time on her hands leaves her with too much time to worry about my every move."

I was mad because there was a black woman out there lucky enough to find a man who offered to financially support her every dream and somehow managed not to have any. I was crying in a sense, not only for me but for all the straight-up wonderful, ambitious, struggling, and single sistas I knew—women who had dreams and mad love to give but could barely find brothers willing to listen. Sistas who, I knew, if given the opportunity this brother was providing, would give a heartfelt thanks to the Creator—and then show Him how high they can fly.

I was crying because an admittedly frightened, weak, vulnerable, but oh so real part of me wanted to yell, *"TAKE CARE OF ME. PROTECT ME. BE THERE FOR ME.*

LOVE ME." Instead, I ended the last conversation we would have for two years by calling him everything but a child of God.

It's not fair, BethAnn. It's just not fair.

"I know, sweetheart. That's why it hurts so much. 'Cuz us smart, good-hearted, independent girls, we're the best. We're out there handling our business and conquering the world, and we manage to be there for them too. We've got their backs. We're the ones they call in the middle of the night. We're like their best friends. The only thing we ask for is for them to be their best. And then it's the weak ones who do the things we wouldn't dream of—"

Like getting pregnant on purpose.

"Right. Threatening to kill yourself. You know, the things we would never do. And those are the girls who seem to win.

"But, baby?"

Yes, BethAnn.

"They don't win forever. They really don't. You're young so it seems like that now. But remember, we mature faster than boys. Sometimes it takes the men we love a little longer to realize how much they love us."

I hung up the phone, hoping to God she was right.

• • •

I hear you, the non-believers, steadily testifying. *Not me. Not I. There's nothing I could possibly have in common, let alone envy, about a chickenhead.* And for a precious few sista-saints this might actually be true. The rest of you, my dears, are fronting. Not to worry, though. Chickenhead Envy is usually accompanied by intense denial.

To you I offer my favorite Chickenhead litmus test: a piece of entertainment industry gossip concerning a certain celebrity. Contrary to his image as a family man, rumor has it the brother's been tipping—albeit discreetly—on longtime wifey for years. His tipping wasn't hard to fathom—baby must have more money than God and is 'bout as fine as Jesus. With his mega-fame, extramarital ass is a given on his menu in just about any country with a working TV. What would wifey's incentive be for turning a blind eye? Maybe a combination of love, being the mother of his children, and landing in the mix pre-fame and without a good pre-nup.

What I couldn't get was how he would manage to keep his shit so on the low. As the old saying goes, *Hell hath no fury like a woman pissed off.* In addition to wreaking a little domestic havoc and tarnishing his image, any scorned mistress of his stood to make a bundle confiding the details of her heartbreak to the media.

So needless to say, when one of my homeboys said he discovered much fewer than six degrees of separation between himself and one of Mr. Mention's alleged mistresses, I was wide open on the details. Word is, according to my boy, he goes through great pains to make silence and loyalty a helluva lot more lucrative than kissing and telling. "All I can tell you is that he treats her very, very well. The car, house, and living expenses are all taken care of—plus an allowance in six figures a year. And Joan, are you ready for this? She's not the only one."

The next time I see Mr. Mention on TV all I can think is *Damn. Another million for the ho fund.* Then I find myself envisioning the lucky chicken chillin' in a new Mercedes SLK Kompressor and discover something else —envy-green is an unattractive shade for an allegedly righteous black girl. Curious to see other sistas' reactions, I repeated this "what if" scenario.

The results of my informal poll? With the exception of one admirable saint (and she wasn't me) we all failed to take the high road. The only difference was that girlfriends who were unabashed graduates of "Pussy

Ain't Free U" weren't hampered by things like moral quandaries or my womanist drivel. All they wanted to know, in the succinct words of one, was *Where are the auditions?* My chickenhead-hatin' homegirls, however, did a lot more qualifying.

His wife is cool about it, right? I mean she's gotta know.

I wouldn't do it if I was in love.

And my favorite,

I wouldn't do it for like $50,000 or something 'cuz you could really make that on your own—but $300,000— where's a black woman gonna make that kinda money legally? It's not like you'd be selling out for a couple of pairs of Manolo Blahniks. We're talking major lifestyle change.

And moi? Let's just say thoughts of my late mortgage payment, the new paint job my co-op could definitely stand, and the still-to-be-paid-for elite degree that was supposed to give me the keys to the world, temporarily clouded my vision. *I wouldn't do it forever. Three and a half years would be plenty. And I'd quit in a second if I fell in love.* Then shockingly remorseless, I envisioned the all-female film and music production company I could run.

Of course, what we'd *do* if the reality hit might be quite different from speculation, but the reactions confirmed something I've long suspected—given the right circumstances even righteous sistas can be tempted to get their "cluck, cluck" on.

So why in these days of considerable female advances does a bit of the chicken live on, even in the best of us? The reasons are ultimately rooted in society's good ol' sexist imbalance of power. Despite women's considerable gains in economic, social, and political terrains, the gatekeepers to power are still men. This is particularly true for black women. Feminism, degrees, hard work—it's all good—but when it comes to six figure and above lifestyles most of the ballers are men.

Unfortunately, power is still divided by gender. And in a world where *men got the lucci and we got the coochie,* the one self-inflicted Achilles' heel men have is their tendency to define power partially in terms of sexual conquest. Punanny is the one thing women *control* and men have an unlimited desire for. That makes it, even in these post-feminist times, one helluva negotiating tool. "Trickin' "—specifically using sex (or the suggestion of it) to gain protection, wealth, and power—is a feminine device probably as old as sexism itself. From chickenheads to feminists, most women possess an almost intuitive understanding of the role sex, money, and power play in our intimate relationships—and we accommodate accordingly.

The phenomenal commercial success of rappers Foxy Brown and Lil' Kim—the official chickenhead patron saints—are one example. Unlike MC Lyte, Queen Latifah, Salt-N-Pepa, or Yo Yo, Kim and Foxy are hardly examples of Afro-femme regality, refined sensuality, or womanist strength. These baby girls—with their history-making multi-platinum debuts—have the lyrical personas of hyper-sexed, couture-clad hoochie mamas. Once again hip-hop holds up its unwanted mirror and drives home a little-discussed truth. In these days of Cristal, Versace, and Benjamin-filled illusions, the punanny-for-sale materialism which dominates Kim's and Foxy's albums runs rampant in the black community—and it cuts across age and class lines. The same sistas who boogied through the eighties singing "Ain't Nothing Going On but the Rent" were the ones up in arms about their daughters singing "No money, money, no licky, licky. Fuck the dicky, dicky" along with Lil' Kim. Ironic, since both sentiments reduce a brother's value to what's in his wallet.

For many women trickin' is less a matter of right or wrong, than an issue of personal taste and context. Des,* for example, a receptionist in her early thirties,

* Not her real name.

thinks Kim and Foxy are shamelessly "nasty little girls," but she has no problem telling the BMWs that park in her lot to "show her the money." With flawless taste and impeccable grooming, Des is not only as fine as she wants to be, she's the kind of woman whose entrance effortlessly brings the room to a pause. She prides herself on being the definitive trophy girl—good looks, great body, and the ability to "make any man I'm with feel like it's *all* about him." It's a well-cultivated talent she feels her man should pay for. "I'm not greedy, but when it comes to things like clothes, or taking care of myself, I have no problems asking them for money. Let's face it—this takes money and time. If they like the way I look, then they need to help pay for the maintenance."

What it takes her men longer to see is that Des is also smart, driven, and ambitious. Moonlighting as a stylist, she hopes to have her own business one day. But after sharing her dream with several boyfriends, she found herself hurt and disappointed. Even though "they could more than afford it" they refused to invest in her business. "What killed me is they knew I could do it," she says angrily. "Half the clients I work with now are ones I got through them. The funny thing is that when it came to buying me jewelry, furs, or paying my rent, they had no problems. But when it came to my business, it was always some tired excuse. The bottom line was, they weren't trying to do anything that would empower *me* and let me do for myself."

So now Des "takes no shorts." Her current boyfriend —wealthy and married—was told in no uncertain terms that she would only see him if he deposited several hundred dollars in the bank every first of the month. For Des, it's not about love or trickin'. She simply sees it as a way of making sure the relationship also serves her "best interests." "I'm not about to be one of these ridiculous women who sits around waiting for her married boyfriend to leave his wife, while he has his cake and eats it too. I know a married man with kids isn't capable of giving me the kind of support, time, or dedication I'd require in a full-time relationship. So in the meantime, I'm trying to build something that's going to secure my future. That money goes straight to my business."

For most of us, however, the negotiation rarely plays itself out in a strictly monetary exchange. Trickin' is often a less straightforward affair—the more subtle, the more socially acceptable. It's the persuasive, silent "punanny strike" you go on 'til your honey comes 'round and sees things your way. "Not giving it up" until you've gotten at least one present and a few nice dinners. That amnesia-inspiring flirtation you reflexively bestow on a male traffic officer if you bust him stealing appreciative glances at your breasts. The power suit with the notably short skirt you save for meetings with those executive boys. At its essence, trickin' is a woman's ability to use her looks, femininity, and flirtation to gain advantage in an inarguably sexist world.

Its intractability, however, speaks to something far more complex than mere female strategy, greed, or sexual manipulation. Trickin's prevalence across class lines demonstrates just how deeply wedded money, sex, and power are to our notions of male and female identity.

Comedian Chris Rock once asked me to talk him through the nuances of courting a feminist woman. "Would it offend her if I paid?" My answer, I thought, was tight. *Of course you should pay. I think a lot of guys don't understand what being a feminist means. Just because I'm a feminist doesn't mean I'm not a woman. And sometimes women like to feel nurtured and special and feel like they're being taken care of.*

Besides, it's just good home training.

"So paying is good home training?"

Definitely. If you ask a woman out you should pay. And then in a futile attempt at equanimity, I added smugly, *And you know what, Chris, if I asked you out I would pay.*

Then he blew up my spot. "You would pay? Now you know that's bullshit. You might act like you're going to pay. You might have your money in your pocket and reach like you were ready to pay. But the second I *let* you pay you would never go out with me again."

He was right. I couldn't remember the last time I'd put my hand in my pocketbook even on a second or third date—let alone a first. I wasn't brought up this way. Moms was not an advocate of trickin' in any form. The many years she was forced to postpone her dreams —college, a career, travel—essentially because my father refused to come home from work and help take care of small children, left too many footprints on her spirit. She got to college by working as a domestic, taking whatever could be salvaged out of $2.00 an hour after raising three kids, and stuffing her dreams into an old thermos bottle. By the time her youngest was in junior high, there was finally enough money for her tuition. My father never gave her a penny.

Her experiences informed the brief but very specific rules I was given when it came to boys and dating.

1. No accepting gifts of monetary value.
2. If he pays first, you pay second and try to go Dutch as often as possible.
3. Never, ever, ever, leave home without your feisty (Jamaican for "rude") money—enough change for a phone call, and if not taxi fare then at least two tokens.

When asked to explain the whys of it all, my mother's only comment was "God bless the child that's got her own." So while I collected poems, love letters, and flowers, my fellow ghetto princesses stuffed their closets with designer clothes, gold chains, and expensive sneakers.

It never dawned on me that sex figured prominently into this equation until one day, while longingly admiring my friend Tai's* most recent acquisitions (among them a slamming new pair of Anne Klein loafers) I ventured to ask exactly *how* her seventeen-year-old non-working and living in the projects behind could afford it all. She could not believe my naïveté. "Girl, my man gets it for me." Then thinking of the ass-whooping I'd be sure to get if I tried to do the same, I asked what in

* Not her real name.

the world she told her mom. "My motha is the one who told me," she said. *"Pussy ain't free.* Don't be giving up my shit to these niggas unless they give me something."

By the time I got to college, I saw that sentiment was hardly limited to the 'hood. There were plenty of sistas whose theme song for relationships shoulda been Janet Jackson's "What Have You Done for Me Lately." Still, I never regretted my mom's advice. Thanks to her, I escaped much of the sexual pressure that plagued many of my peers. For some girls, the deciding factor for whether or not a guy deserved the boots was how much he spent on the courtship process. Unfortunately, the decisions weren't always based on the woman's desires. Very often the more money a guy spent the more he felt he was entitled sexually—and he applied pressure accordingly. Sadly enough, many women complied—not because they wanted to have sex but because they felt that was the price they paid for someone treating them nicely.

That sense of obligation was foreign to me. Since my mother's value system never taught me to make a connection between sex and dollars, it never occurred to me to base my decisions about sex on anything but my desires. A brother was no more likely to get laid if he spent $100 on dinner than if he spent $30 on cab fare and a movie. And no less likely if he didn't.

It wasn't until I grew older, however, and watched women repeatedly relinquish happiness to men who were controlling, disrespectful, and abusive for the sake of "maintaining a certain lifestyle," did I fully recognize my mother's sagacity. In her own silent way, she instilled the importance of financial independence, self-reliance, and determination so her only daughter would know that her heart, soul, spirit, and body were simply not for sale.

For the most part, I am my mother's child. While financial stability and a career he loves are definitely among my dating prerequisites, they matter more to me as indications of a brother's capacity for passion, commitment, and a solid work ethic than what I think his money will do for me. And when it comes to not giving me the respect I think I deserve, money is not a factor I'm ever tempted to place over love or happiness. There've been six- and seven-figure brothers who've suffered the same fate as the ones who were barely getting by. And I'm grateful to my moms for giving me that freedom.

Still, there are plenty of times when those liberated principles get conveniently played to the left. Unfortunately, my mother's well-intentioned, egalitarian approach to dating didn't translate well into the adult, post-college world. Even though the values are intact —I still enjoy treating a brother to dinner or surprising him with a home-cooked meal—I gave up the "Dutch" habit long ago. It was more trouble than it was worth.

To my surprise, if a brother was feeling insecure about his financial status, the offer only ended up making him feel worse. Despite my protestations that it didn't matter—I *liked* when he cooked or we enjoyed a quiet day in his modest studio—all it took was one three-day assignment with some member of the Black Boy Millionaire Club, or some investment banker I knew to glance at him the wrong way and we'd be back to the same old nonsense. *I don't know why you even fucking with me. You should be with some nigga that can give you the world.*

Even if the financials and confidence were clearly intact, most brothers viewed my insistence on splitting the bill as anything from unnecessary to annoying.

In my honest confusion, and my desire not to join the ranks of irate sistas who honestly feel like *brothers just can't deal with independent black women* I went and sought the counsel of my homeboys. Invariably they told me the same thing. Just because a man's ability to pay wasn't an issue for me it did not mean it wasn't an issue for him.

The point was driven home one night by this cutie in San Francisco. Despite being told each time we went out that he'd "never let a lady pay," I'd instinctively reach for my wallet. This time, however, he'd gone to great lengths to plan a particularly romantic evening and the gesture came dangerously close to ruining it. Baby read me the riot act. *Why do you always do that? I already know you're an independent woman. That's why I'm here. But damn, Joan, a man needs to feel like he can do for a woman. And when you tell a brother you won't even let him pay for a meal, it's like you don't want to be vulnerable at all.*

Then, responding to that silent, pouty twelve-year-old thing I do whenever I'm effectively called out, he gently took my hand. *Look. I admit it. I need to feel needed. And I think you could use some taking care of. So why don't you let that superwoman shit go for a minute and let a brother do his thing?*

He did have a point. The teenager my mom sought to protect by devising those rules was now a fully grown woman. Her values were already too deeply ingrained for me to really be at risk. I already knew that a man paying for dinner, a hotel, or an airline ticket did not entitle him to a piece of my ass. And truth be told, the same ultra-independent STRONG-BLACKWOMANisms that compelled me to go Dutch were also the ones that landed me in Frisco in the first place—tired, unhappy, and sick of my life. Besides, at that very moment, staring into those big baby browns was far more important to me than my mother's advice or feminism. I conceded. I never tried to pay on one of our dates again. Eventually I gave the practice up altogether.

My mother's approach wasn't wrong, it was just short-sighted. Like so many God-blessed girl children raised to have their own, I was naively unrealistic about the effect economic and professional disparities can have on a relationship. Call it the aftereffect of growing up in a cultural amalgam of Protestant work ethic *(Hard work is next to Godliness)*, capitalism *(It's all about the Benjamins, baby)*, social Darwinism *(Only the strongest/richest survive)*. American men tend to invest a great deal of their identity and self-worth in what they do, how much they make, and their ability to provide. For many, it's an intrinsic part of how they define their manhood.

For black men, racism greatly intensifies this reality. As far back as emancipation, black men assumed that the ability to acquire wealth and property would decrease the emasculating impact of racism. Even though Booker T. Washington's anti-integrationist advice to the masses to "cast down your buckets where you are" and W. E. B. Du Bois's dreams of a "Talented Tenth" —a fully integrated black leadership elite—were seemingly at odds, both leaders embraced the same premise: that hard, honorable work could win black folks a certain degree of legitimacy in an otherwise hostile society.

More than a century later, that sentiment is still prevalent. According to Keith T. Clinkscales, successful BMW and president and C.E.O. of *Vibe,* "Black men are very often characterized by the media, society, popular fiction as not being 'real men.' We're depicted as not providing for our families or doing our thing. And believe me, nobody wants to have that on them. Brothers want to handle their business. They want to prove to themselves and everyone else, that they are real men."

While he believes that it's impossible to escape racism, Clinkscales maintains that a certain degree of "professional achievement does provides black men with the state of mind necessary to combat racism more effectively.

"It's not necessarily even an issue of how much you

make. Money may become a barometer of success in certain professions, like your Wall Street professions, but I think for a lot of brothers, it's more about just wanting to be good. The belief is that if you can just enjoy what you do and be really good at it, then you have a great chance at making money."

Paul Jacobs,* a professional athlete and fledgling entrepreneur, echoes Clinkscales's sentiments strongly. "As a black man, professional success validates you and gives you the ability to compete, especially against the white men of the world. It's like your check."

Women, however, have a very different barometer of worth. Thanks to sexism, there is considerably less pressure on us to be financially and professionally successful. For better or worse, society still allows us to measure our overall worth in ways that have nothing to do with our careers, like being good mothers, wives, or community workers. The pressure we feel about our ability to make paper is usually more about economic survival, dreams, and ambition than maintaining our "feminine" identity.

A lot of times what black women perceive to be

* Not his real name.

brothers' "inability to deal with independent women" is really their struggle with a culture that views men who are less than financially solid as something "less than men."

"You know, I hear a lot of strong, intelligent women say they intimidate brothers," says Clinkscales. "I think that they do intimidate some. But if they do, then there's a good chance that's not the guy they really need to be with. Smart, together sistas need to be with the type of man who is fearless, courageous, and wants to succeed badly enough that he'll jump into any situation."

He does caution, however, that a brother's desire for success in not necessarily indicative of his confidence level. "There are a lot of insecurities that come with trying to succeed. There's an intense amount of pressure to make it. Some brothers may seem like they have a lot of confidence, but sometimes it's just not real."

While Jacobs doesn't buy that brothers are necessarily intimidated by strong women, he does think that sistas need to be more realistic about what they're up against. "It's rare for a woman to find a guy that can deal with the completely assed out feeling that comes with being broke or just not being where you want to be. The bottom line is, as a man in this world, not having paper makes you feel weak and vulnerable. Your girl could even be Willy—fine, paper, and status—*and* not care. It still wouldn't matter. The second she takes you out in her circles and you gotta be around other niggas with jobs and status, it's not cool anymore. The second anybody wants to know what you do, you feel like a pumpkin."

Complicating these feelings of insecurity are male competition and ego. What Jacobs affectionately calls "the whole rooster thing. . . . In a room full of roosters, the strongest rooster wins. And if your shit is not right you are definitely gonna have to watch other roosters with paper and status try to get at your girl. They're sending her bouquets of flowers and you can't even give her a rose."

Still, Jacobs maintains it's not all about the men. He attributes a lot of brothers' inability to flow under those circumstances to what he perceives to be most *women's* materialism. From his experience, a sista's claim to be satisfied with "a quality guy with good morals, upbringing, and potential" is usually "bullshit."

"When most women say they recognize a brother's potential, it's really just a smoke screen. Because if the potential doesn't rise as fast as *they* think it should, they keep right on moving. For a woman to be loyal even when it seems like it's the darkest hour—when it's like *Goddamn, another peanut butter and jelly sandwich*—is very, very rare.

"The bottom line is this: Women *like* to be taken out. They *like* to be with men who have status in their social circles. And they want to be with a guy with some money and at least a little bit of power."

Sad but true. As liberated women we may revel in our ability to pay our own way but we're not likely to fall for the men who let us. The one boyfriend I had who actually took the "feminist" approach of splitting all our dating expenses—everything from the movies to vacations—squarely down the middle, couldn't win for trying. Since he made almost three times my salary, my "feminist" mind had trouble processing his actions as anything but cheap. Hypocritical as it was, the sight of him calculating the bill had the undesirable effect of waterhosing my libido.

Let's face it, money and the ability to spend it freely is one of society's strongest assertions of power—and power is a very sexy thing. There's an undeniable, take-charge sex appeal that a man has when he's trickin' loot. Whether it's game or not, when a man picks up the tab he gives the impression of being able to "handle his"—himself, his affairs, and his woman.

"Sometimes, it's not a power or an ego thing," says Jacobs—who, for the record, *always* pays. More often than not, he explains, a brother's ability to trick loot on a woman he likes simply makes him feel like a good guy. "It's one of the ways we're taught to be a gentleman. You pay—even if you know she can pay for herself. It's like walking on the outside of the street, you know that nothing's probably gonna happen but you do it anyway. Or opening the door even though you know she can open it herself. It's just the gentlemanly, chivalrous thing to do."

Men have long figured out what us liberated supasistas have been loath to admit: Men are not the only ones with a vested interest in sexism. When it comes to equality, most of us are only willing to go but so far. Equal pay for equal work, yes. Equal access and opportunity, certainly. But complete and total equality? Not hardly. Because while we recognize sexism's evils, we also fully enjoy its privileges—not least among them chivalry.

Gender-biased it may be, but in a society of ever-shifting gender roles, temporarily indulging the men lucci/women coochie division of power offers a soothing semblance of order. Not to wax nostalgic for the "good old days" but those much-needed feminist advances also left our generation disconcertingly bewil-

dered about what our "roles" are as men and women—
and how they relate to each other. As a result, women's
struggle for political, economic, and social equality has
always been infinitely clearer than the internal battle
we wage trying to honor both our independence and
our femininity. Dating is one of the few areas in my life
that I get to completely indulge the latter. For a few
hours I don't *want* equality. I want the door held open,
the chair pulled out, and I don't want to think about
money at all. I want nothing more than the ultra-femme
responsibility of juggling hairstylist and mani/pedi appointments, being a great conversationalist, and looking
like a dime.

Ironically this is probably more symptomatic of feminism than an abandonment of it. As much as I enjoy
the challenge of kicking ass at work, paying the bills,
staying fit, staying sane, and leaping tall buildings in a
single bound, letting a man spend a little dough ex-
presses the "feminine" desire to let somebody else take
care of *me* for a change.

Just call it the "chicken" in me.

Until the day we find ourselves in the throes of a
feminist revolution, trickin' isn't likely to go away.
Whatever our disdain for chickenheads may be, it's

obvious that trickin' is too intricately woven into our culture's social fabric to simply tell baby girls to "Just Say No." We live in a world where strippers out-earn women with college degrees and antiquated alimony and child-support laws guarantee some women higher standards of living than most 9 to 5's ever could. Chickens rely on punanny for the same reasons drug dealers don't struggle through four years of college: In a world of limited resources, trickin' is a viable means of elevating one's game.

Truth be told, there are a few things we could learn from our chickenhead sistren. When it comes to maximizing the resources the good Lord gave 'em, girlfriends are nice with theirs. Chickens *always* look good. They don't drop their drawers unless there's something valuable to garner out of the exchange. And they recognize the intrinsic value in occasionally allowing a man "to just be a man." Basically, chickenheads accept that in a male-dominated society obsessed with both beauty and sex, there is something to be said for women effectively working their erotic power.

Rapper/actress Queen Latifah would tend to agree. Despite a great deal of public pressure she refused "to chastise Kim and Foxy" for their sexually explicit lyrics. "A lot of [women] were really on that bandwagon," she said, "but I think we need to get over ourselves. Queen down, we've all got our share of shit in the closet, so why act holier than thou? Somebody is finally saying it in plain English: If you cum then I'm gonna cum. If he's gonna get what he wants then I'm gonna get what I want. And these are not unlike things I say myself.

"Who am I to tell Kim to put some clothes on?" she continued. "Or to say that she needs to stop talking about money and jewels? I understand that she wants that. I want those things too. We just go about getting it in different ways.

"Kim sees her power in a different way than I see my power," she reasons. "And she may feel that she's working her power to the best of her ability—instead of letting somebody else pimp that power.

"And let's face it, men have been pimping pussy power for a very, very, long time.

"The bottom line," she concludes, "is that pussy is a powerful thing. And I've come to recognize that some women can use it to gain things for themselves because they see it as their greatest strength."

Not all women are as comfortable with erotic power as Queen Latifah. There are sistas like Danni,* who find the idea of women exploiting the competitive edge

* Not her real name.

society grants attractive *people* complicit and offensive. "It's not fair," says the thirty-something film production coordinator, who, by the way, got her share of good looks and somebody else's. "When it comes to work, I don't think looks should have any relevance. I've been in situations where I was one of two women up for a position and I was chosen—knowing that the other person may be slightly more qualified. It bothers me that I got the job because some man decided I was better for him to look at every day."

Still, she admits it never bothered her "enough to *not* take the job." Her friend Shawn,* a self-described feminist with absolutely no chickenhead envy (in addition to being the breadwinner, her husband does all the cooking and supports her fledgling film career) thinks Danni should cut herself some slack. She points out an interesting double standard: Smart, personable, attractive men rely on their combined attributes all the time to advance themselves socially and professionally—and call it charm. Women who do the same, however, are accused by others of "selling out." The fear is that playing these games place all but the most attractive women at a disadvantage.

But women who feel this way about erotic power

* Not her real name.

have it terribly misconstrued. "Erotic power isn't based solely on looks," explains Shawn. "Ultimately, it's about understanding the power of the *feminine* and your power as a woman. There are women who are not what you would consider conventionally attractive who are very good at working their feminine power. And I think it's time feminism let women know that using that power is okay—instead of demeaning or ridiculing them."

Liz,* a southern belle and a bit of a feminist femme fatale, is also down with erotic power. Being fully in command of one's womanly charms, she maintains, is a powerful tool when it comes to battling sexism. She calls it working the "militant feminine." "Oh, if you're a guy and you're putting me in a sexist situation, I'm sorry for you," warns the thirty-something costume designer. "Because I *love* that power.

"I'm strong enough and old enough to see that when it comes to getting what I want from men I don't have to be *right* all the time," she explains. "I'd really rather win.

"Some of the most successful women in life know that the more attention you give men, the farther you're going to get. He could be wrong or talking

* Not her real name.

about something really stupid but they know how to make their point in a way that doesn't put it up all in his face." Doing this doesn't make her feel angry or compromised at all. "I'm such a strong, militantly feminine person," she says proudly, "that I'm into it."

Liz and Shawn are poignant examples of how women today differ from their foremothers. In the past, feminists were understandably loath to condone utilizing erotic power as a means of battling sexism. Many remembered all too vividly a time when erotic power was all women had—and it was rarely enough to circumvent abuse and exploitation.

But while women today still experience sexism, we do so in markedly different ways. Many of us are empowered enough to combine our erotic power with resources that were unimaginable to our mothers—money, education, talent, drive, ambition, confidence, and the freedom to just "go for ours."

We have the luxury of choosing both our battles and our artillery. We know that sometimes winning requires utilizing whatever confrontational measures are necessary. We're not afraid of lawsuits, boycotts, organized protests, or giving a deserving offender a good cussing out. But we also recognize that there are times when winning requires a lighter touch. And sometimes a short skirt and a bat of the eyes is not only easier but infinitely more effective.

But before we go casting our liberated principles to the wind and get our "cluck, cluck" on, remember that chickenheads rarely win. When it comes to the division of power, men get a much better deal. With any skill, their power (money) increases exponentially over time. Thanks to deeply embedded prejudices regarding women and aging, ours (coochie and beauty) diminishes drastically with age. More often than not a pretty, young chicken who tricked her way through her twenties may find herself out of the game by thirty. "Successful" chickens are usually a mere fraction of those who ass out trying.

For sistas especially, relying on punanny power to secure one's future is a crapshoot, at best. Given the harsh economic realities of black folks' lives, chickens are up against phenomenal odds. Despite the fairy-tale appeal of Cinderella stories, black Prince Charmings— specifically, brothers making enough paper to set their women comfortably in the lap of luxury—are exceedingly rare. Girlfriends pursuing that prince at the exclusion of all others would be wise to broaden their horizons. As of 1992, the number of blacks (male and female) making $50,000 or more was a pathetic *1 per-*

cent of the African-American population.[1] More often than not, married couples who reached the nirvana of black middle-classdom were only able to do so by *combining* their incomes. Even with the burgeoning of the black middle class and the entertainment industry's highly publicized black millionaires, there simply aren't enough rappers, ball players, doctors, lawyers, or even gainfully employed brothers to satisfy the enormous demand.

Besides, landing the prince doesn't necessarily make a sista empowered. Nicky,* a twenty-seven-year-old doctor once dated an NBA Willy and describes it as one of "the most depressing periods" of her life. Attractive, funny, confident, and intelligent enough to graduate top of her class at Yale medical school, Nicky still found that the infinite number of beautiful women that checked for her man—"everything from that fine-ass R&B singer to the jiggy entertainment lawyer to the hoochie go-go bitch dancing in some cage" played havoc with her self-esteem.

"I never thought I could be that girl but all of a sudden I found myself obsessing about everything. Every day it was like, 'Am I thin enough? Are my titties

* Not her real name.

too small? Is my ass too big? Is my hair too short? Am I too light? Am I light enough?' It was ridiculous. It's a competition you can't possibly win."

Finally, for the sake of her sanity, she decided to cut him loose. "I realized that he just wasn't making me feel secure enough about the relationship to not worry about other women. And if you gotta rely on pretty to keep a man, forget it. No matter how pretty you are there's always going to be someone prettier. No matter how good you can get your freak on, there's always some girl out there who can freak it better."

Nicky's observations drive home the ultimate truth about erotic power. Without financial independence, education, ambition, intelligence, spirituality, and love, punanny alone isn't all that powerful. The reality is that it's easily replaceable, inexhaustible in supply, and quite frankly, common as shit. Women who value their erotic power over everything else stand to do some serious damage to their self-esteem.

Ultimately, the illusion that chickenheads win is fueled by a lack of understanding of how sexism works. Sexism is one instance where it's virtually impossible to dismantle the master's house with the master's tools. No matter how well women think they've mastered the game, they're still playing by somebody else's rules.

And when it comes to women and sex, the old double standards are still very much in effect.

Chris Lighty, Violator Records president and chickenhead fave, is straight-up about it. "It's sexist and it's male chauvinist, but there are a lot of beautiful, nice women who'll end up missing out, just because they've been with too many of us." (Too many by the way, according to Chris, is any number greater than two.) When I point out the hypocrisy in this, that a number of brothers in the Black Boy Millionaire Club sleep with everything in sight, he doesn't even bother denying it. "We all *like* the jiggy freaks and we wanna sleep with her and her friends—maybe even at the same time— but that's just sex," he emphasizes. "That's *not* the girl we marry. None of us wants to be sitting at dinner with Michael Jordan, Puffy, Shaquille O'Neal, and the new hot rapper and know they've been with your girl."

His answer brings back BethAnn's parting words to me that fateful day she talked me through my Chickenhead Envy. *They don't win forever. It just takes the men we love a little longer to realize how much they love us.*

Curious, I ask Lighty if he thinks this is true. "You're asking me if chickenheads win?" He laughs good and hard at the question. "No, of course they don't. If they win it's only for a minute. Chickenheads are like a temporary ego boost. We know it doesn't take much to get a chicken. All you need is a good watch and a little bit of cash. And for a man, there's no real victory in that."

I also ask Puff Daddy, aka Sean Combs. Essentially he says the same thing. When it comes to wifey, it seems, chickens will not do at all. Even though the multi-millionaire mogul/pop star can more than provide, he's not checking for providing chickens with a life of leisure. "Don't get me wrong," he explains, "I want to provide for my woman, but at the same I want a woman that's ambitious. A motivator, one that's going to make the team stronger.

"I want us to be partners blowing up together," he continues. "And I *want* her to get her ass out of bed before twelve in the afternoon because I *work* until five in the morning. I should not wake up and see my woman in bed sleeping. Write a screenplay. Build a school in Africa. Do *something.* I *don't* want a woman who would have me be up all night *busting my ass* and not even want to cook me breakfast 'cuz she's waiting for the maid."

What about the big-ass-big-titties-and-jiggy-good looks?

"Yeah, I'm looking for fly and beautiful," he sighs. "But it's not just about that look good shit. Really. That wears thin no matter what. You can find something wrong with the prettiest girl after you've been looking at her for a couple of months. I want a woman that's strong."

Clinkscales can't even believe I'm asking the question. "Men who are successful in life," he offers quietly, "appreciate intelligent and thoughtful women—I think much more than women know. When we're looking for the long term, those are the qualities we want. Not chickenheads.

"Now I admit that a lot of this understanding for men comes with age," he concedes, "but all that aesthetic stuff goes away really quickly. As you get older, what's beautiful to you really transforms. Aesthetic beauty is one thing, but I can't even tell you how beautiful a woman is who has a soothing, calm personality in a world that's otherwise hectic and completely ridiculous.

"And she gets more beautiful as things go on."

P.S. Ms. Chicken. Eat your heart out.

one last thing
before I go

I know that ours has never been an easy relationship. Sistahood ain't sainthood. That nonsense about if women had power there would be no wars is feminist delusion at best. We might not get down with guns and bombs but when it comes to emotional carnage we can be quite brutal with ours. Ain't a black woman alive who hasn't experienced the jealousy, duplicity, backstabbing, and competitiveness sistas are capable of. This is especially true when racism and sexism's got us convinced that there just ain't enough happiness to go around. So while we go ahead and kill each other over one tiny-ass slice of the American pie, the white boys walk away with the lion's share.

That being said, know that when it comes to sistahood, I am deadly serious about my commitment to you. The communal bonds forged by shared historical, cultural, and spiritual experiences have made us fam. As long as inequality and oppression remain constants in our lives, sistahood is critical to our mutual survival. We owe it to each other (and the yet shortys to come) to encourage other sistas through the doors we've passed through. Giving the gift of our survival experiences freely is part of the debt we owe to the sistas who battled not only for their empowerment, but our own.

The quest for power is not a solo trip. This book only starts the journey. Only you can complete it.

See you when we get there.

Joan

source notes

intro.: dress up

1. Joan Morgan, "Baby's Mama," *Essence,* August 1997, p. 85.

hip-hop feminist

1. Kristal Brent-Zooks, "A Manifesto of Sorts for a New Black Feminist Movement," *The New York Times Magazine,* November 12, 1995, p. 86.
2. Ibid, pp. 88–89.

from fly-girls to bitches and hos

1. Michelle Wallace, "When Black Feminism Faces the Music, and the Music Is Rap," *The New York Times,* July 29, 1990.

2. Joan Morgan, "Real Love," *Vibe,* April 1996, p. 38.

3. Kevin Powell, "The Vibe Q: Tupac Shakur, Ready to Live," *Vibe,* April 11, 1995, p 52.

strongblackwomen

1. Michele Wallace, *Black Macho and the Myth of the Superwoman* (New York: Dial Press, 1978), p. 153.

2. Paula Giddings, *Where and When I Enter: The Impact of Race and Sex on America* (New York: William Morrow, 1984), p. 43.

3. Ibid.

4. Ibid., p. 31.

5. Wallace, *Black Macho,* p. 107.

6. Ibid., p. 107.

7. Ibid.

8. Diane Marie Weathers, "Death of a Superwoman," *Essence,* March 1998, p. 84.

9. The Sentencing Project, "Young Black Americans & the Criminal Justice System: Five Years Later," October 1995.

10. Farai Chideya, *Don't Believe the Hype: Fighting Cultural Misinformation About African-Americans* (New York: Plume, 1995), pp. 16 and 117.

strongblackwomen -n- endangeredblackmen . . .
this is not a love story

1. Chideya, op. cit., p. 21.

2. Ibid.

3. Marita Golden, *Saving Our Sons: Raising Black Children in a Turbulent World* (New York: Doubleday, 1995), pp. 11–12.

4. Dr. Jawanza Kunjufu, "Turning Boys into Men," *Essence,* November 1988, p. 112.

5. Golden, *Saving Our Sons,* pp. 187–188.

babymother

1. Michele Ingrassia, "Endangered Family," *Newsweek,* August 30, 1993, pp. 17–18.

2. Joan Morgan, "Baby's Mama," *Essence,* August 1997, p. 85.

3. Ingrassia, "Endangered Family," p. 21.

4. Ibid., p. 18.

5. Mary Frances Berry, *The Politics of Parenthood* (New York: Random House, 1995), p. 218.

6. Ellis Cose, *A Man's World: How Real Is Male Privilege—and How High Is Its Price?* (New York: HarperCollins, 1995), p. 163.

7. Ibid., p. 182.

8. Ibid.

9. Ibid, p. 180.

chickenhead envy

1. Farai Chideya, *Don't Believe the Hype,* pp. 17 and 117.

index

WHEN CHICKENHEADS COME HOME TO ROOST

1. Morgan says that, more than any other generation before, this generation needs a feminism committed to "keeping it real." How does this translate day-to-day, person-to-person? Is it possible for a woman to be a good feminist and not pay for her own dinner, not hold the door open, or not become a master mechanic, as Morgan's feminism prescribes? Are you a feminist? What does Morgan mean when she says that "the empowerment of the black community [has] to include its women" or that "sexism [stands] stubbornly in the way of black men and women loving each other or sistas loving themselves"?

2. Hip-hop and rap have come under attack lately on many fronts. Is it possible to like this music despite the fact that it contains so much misogyny? Are you able to listen to the music and use it as a tool to understand how the community works, as Morgan advocates, or would it be better to silence its violent content?

3. Morgan says, "We're all winners when space exists for brothers to honestly state and explore the roots of their pain and subsequently their misogyny, sans judgment." Besides rap and hip-hop, what are some effective ways, or forums, in which black men and women can "lovingly address the uncomfortable issues of [their] failing self-esteem, the ways [they] sexualize and objectify [themselves, and their] confusion about sex and love"? How about ways to address the "unhealthy, unloving, unsisterly" ways black women treat one another? What are some things you regret doing, and how would you change your words and actions?

4. The author says that, by consenting to appear in raunchy music videos, certain women only promote sexist images of themselves and that there will always be women who trade on their sexuality to get the person (or the "protection, wealth, and power") they want. Do you agree that young black women share in the responsibility for hip-hop's antiwomen attitudes? Do you believe that women who value their erotic power over all else stand to seriously damage their self-esteem? Are there other ways, besides trading on sex, to attract the opposite sex? Is there a bit of Chickenhead in all of us?

5. What do you think of Morgan's notion that the popular urban myth of the "ENDANGEREDBLACKMAN" (EBM) should also apply to black women, who suffer from breast cancer and AIDS and poverty and incarceration at rates much greater than white women? What does Morgan mean when she states that ENDANGEREDBLACKMEN *"succumb* to being ENDANGERED" and that "EBM are wholly incompatible with daughters raised to be strong women"?

6. Does the notion of the "STRONGBLACKWOMAN" empower you or oppress you? Do you agree that contemporary black women perpetuate the myth of the STRONGBLACKWOMAN to boost their fractured self-esteems? How do they do this? Do you believe that black men are less capable of surviving the afflictions of life than black women?

7. Throughout the book, the author emphasizes that lack of respect is a problem that plagues the black community. Do black women love, yet not respect, black men? What do you think of Morgan's idea that women shouldn't spend time with other women who don't respect men and that "participating in . . . men-bashing sessions means . . . commiserating with sistas who are just as clueless as [you are] about how to have a healthy relationship"?

8. Since black women have provided everything for their families for so long, is there any room to believe that men can be relied on and won't drop the ball? What can mothers do to affect their sons' abilities to respect women? Author Marita Golden says, "The generations-old backlog of anger that African-American men and women hoard and revisit and unleash upon one another . . . becomes a script that our sons and daughters memorize. . . . Only when our sons and daughters know that forgiveness is real, existent, and that those who love them practice it, can they form bonds as men and women that really can save and change our community." How can we practice forgiving one another? Can you forgive someone today?

9. Morgan implies that one of the reasons there are so many black women heading single-parent families is because they feel they have little chance of being a part of a traditional two-parent family. Do you agree? Is having a child something you have to do because you have no choice? Do you agree that people should be having discussions with their partners about whether or not they want to have children before they sleep together? If they can't even discuss it, should they even be having sex? What are some ways two people can open a dialogue about this?

10. What are "male reproductive rights"? Why is it so easy to condemn men for not offering full support when they find out that a woman they've been with is pregnant? Can you imagine what it would be like to be pregnant by a man whose child you don't want but he does, and to not have any say about it?

11. Morgan was told that black women don't have time for feminism (or don't "have time for all that shit," to be exact). Where does this ambivalence toward feminism come from? Is it an outgrowth of "black women's historic tendency to blindly defend any black man who seems to be under attack from white folks"? Do you agree that "acknowledging the rampant sexism in [the black] community . . . means relinquishing the comforting illusion that black men and women are a unified front"?

12. In the chapter "STRONGBLACKWOMEN," the author shares a Yoruba fable that helped her figure out what she needed to make her happy. Have you had to learn how to put your needs first, as Morgan did? Can you share some ways that you have done this?